HOW TO BE
A SUCCESSFUL EMCEE

by

LeRoy Stahl

Publishers

T. S. DENISON & COMPANY

Minneapolis

Library of Congress Catalog Card Number: 53-7362

PREFACE

Although this book attempts to be entertaining, it is serious in purpose. For too many years, it has been assumed that a speech need only be natural to be good.

While naturalness may be one of the attributes of a good speech, it is not the only one. There must be form, style, a knowledge of purpose, and a respect for the medium itself. All of these things should go into the making of a speech, if it is to have more than average merit.

The present volume takes it for granted that you already know something about the making of a speech in the ordinary sense; that you know something about the rules of grammar and are able to speak a simple English sentence. What it does try to do is to give you a few useful suggestions in case you are called upon to act as toastmaster or master of ceremonies in an unfamiliar setting.

What it definitely does not try to do is prove that an effective speech will remake your whole personality or counterbalance a lack of vitamins in your diet. Speech-making is a craft, like any other, and it has its uses, like plumbing or the practice of medicine. The ability to make a good speech or to stand on your feet in front of an audience is not necessarily the open sesame to a better life or a chance to marry the boss's daughter.

On the other hand, no apology is made for the concern of this book with what might be termed the lighter phases of the speech field. It may not be as important, for instance, to be a good "straight man" for a comedian as it is to make a world-shaking political speech, but if you are going to do the job at all it should be done well.

If, from time to time, the instructions on the following pages seem picayunish or unduly assertive in their emphasis on craftsmanship and an effort to do a good job, remember that free speech is a vital part of our American heritage. It should be preserved, but, to be preserved, it must also be worthy. If the present book, in however small a way, helps to improve the general quality of the speech work done in the country, it will have served its purpose.

—The Author

CONTENTS

CHAPTER ONE

THE GENERAL IDEA

The job of a master of ceremonies is to present a show, not to be one.

If, like most people, you do not quite know what is expected of you, the first time you are called upon to be a master of ceremonies, you will run like mad to the nearest library. You will try to find a joke book, but the only one available, you discover, was published about the time Teddy Roosevelt and his Rough Riders charged up San Juan Hill. You thumb through its pages, more than a little appalled by what you find there. Yet since you have been called upon to be a master of ceremonies, and a master of ceremonies, you imagine, must be funny, you pick out the least objectionable of the jokes and tell them.

The result almost certainly is a few embarrassed titters from the back of the hall or bewildered looks from the rest of those present. As an embryo master of ceremonies, you either die on the spot or spend the rest of the evening wondering what hit you. Such an impasse results from a misunderstanding, a misconception of function.

The master of ceremonies does not have to be funny. He can be, but his principal job is to take a number of diverse elements and weld them into an entertaining whole.

A Typical Case

Take the average affair at which you, as a beginning master of ceremonies or toastmaster, will be asked to display your wares.

The Society of Petunia Growers in East Fudnuk, Illinois, is holding its annual meeting, at which event a new president will be installed and awards will be presented for the outstanding petunias grown during the year. Dinner is to be served

7

by the Ladies' Aid, and the feature of the evening will be an address by Professor Oliver Ageratum on the subject, "Do Petunias Have a Place in Foreign Affairs?" As an afterthought, a couple of potential juvenile delinquents from the local high school will play a brace of instrumental solos, one on the trombone and the other an arrangement from the works of Bach —for the French horn.

Instead of running to the library, you should sit down quietly with the chairman in charge of arrangements. You should take time to discover exactly what is expected of you and then go over the program again to make certain that nothing is forgotten.

As an additional safeguard, it should be borne in mind that gentlemen—and ladies—in charge of these affairs have a habit of making last-minute changes without consulting the master of ceremonies. Therefore it is the part of wisdom to check informally every day or two to make certain that no such unpleasant surprises are planned for you.

Assuming, though, that everything runs according to plan and that no one comes down with a case of the mumps, you are now faced with the problem of trying to make something out of two instrumental solos, an installation, a presentation of awards, and an address by someone whose talents and capabilities are as yet unknown. It sounds difficult, but it need not be.

Basically what you have are four elements which must be blended into a whole. They must be arranged in such a manner that they lead logically to a climax and at the same time leave room for any co-related material that must be inserted along the way.

Once the ingredients are known, the next step is to take a sheet of paper and number it down the left hand margin with numerals about an inch apart. Then take this skeleton and fill it out with information obtained from the chairman in charge.

There is no magic in this. Its purpose is to enable you to

get a bird's-eye view of the program before you begin. Then, when you have it laid out on a sheet of paper in all its component parts, it is quite easy to make any changes that you desire, and to place one number ahead of the other in any manner that seems to promise better results. Later it may prove desirable to block out the material on separate cards or sheets of paper, but for the moment, it is best to consider the program as a whole.

An Outline

The outline which follows is more complete than is customarily needed, but it gives an idea of what is required for a master of ceremonies successfully to officiate at an entertainment of the type under discussion. The items of the program are given in their chronological order and numbered.

1. Opening Remarks.—It might surprise you to know that it is necessary to tell the assembled petunia growers why they are there. You would think that under the circumstances they would already have this information, but do not depend on it. Someone may have wandered in under the impression that he was attending the funeral of his favorite Aunt Minnie.

Explain in a light and entertaining way that the moment has finally arrived for the petunia growers to take stock of themselves and that later awards will be presented and all hands will be privileged to witness the installation of a new president. Properly done, such a beginning has a tendency to compliment those present for their sagacity in attending such a noteworthy affair, and since you may be a stranger to most of them, it serves in rather a vague way to re-assure the audience that you have some idea of what you are talking about.

Given such a start, your audience is less apt to be disappointed when they fail to get a three-ring circus with all the elephants. Build it up, if you can, but not too much. Get on with the program as fast as possible.

2. Musical Number.—Let the least objectionable of the two musical numbers come second on the program.

The people in front of you have been led to believe that they are going to be bored, at least partially, by something as unprepossessing as a presentation of awards. Instead, you surprise them. You offer something a little bit different.

This is known as the hocus-pocus technique. Nothing here! Nothing there! There is not a great deal with which to work, but by using a little ingenuity, it can be made to sound like a lot.

If the musicians are young and untried—as they inevitably will be—it does no harm for you to see that they get a substantial welcome before they start, making sure that you mention the name of the accompanist, if any. Thank them profusely when they are through. If you are wise, though, you will not let them take more than a single encore, not even if the audience applauds itself into hysteria. Keep the show moving along!

3. **Special Announcements.**—With the performance fairly launched, you can now afford to take a moment or two and thank those who had anything special to do with the arrangements.

Try to include the committee heads. If you can accomplish the job in a light and semi-humorous way, mentioning in a psuedo-derogatory manner some of the characteristics of the persons involved, so much the better. If not, do it straight. Never fail, however, to give them a substantial bit of recognition for their part in the affair, and that means a good round of applause.

Include at this point, also, any other announcements that you may have been asked to make. Sometimes, the sheer quantity of these announcements can get to be laughable but, if you have too many to be handled at one time, it is better to sprinkle them throughout the course of the program.

4. **Presentation of Awards.**—Unless you have a mental lapse of some kind, you will not do this part of the program yourself. You will see to it that someone else gets the job.

Ten to one, though, when the matter is discussed with the program chairman, he will insist that you take on this assignment, too. It will be perfectly easy, he will say, since you are already handling the major part of the program anyway. Don't you believe it! The program chairman is only trying to save himself the task of finding someone else. Be firm. Insist that another person be found. If necessary, go out and find a victim yourself.

It is better to have another speaker make the awards or perform a similar task, because it provides a change in voice and personality. It can get very monotonous, having the same old visage in front of the audience all the time, and a change should be provided.

Besides, if you enlist someone else to do the job, you have an opportunity to collect your thoughts. You do not have to go breathlessly on and introduce the next number the moment you are through. It is enough to introduce the program; you should not have to be a part of it, too.

Choose a person who is well known to the club, or even an outsider will do: a minister, a chamber of commerce secretary, or some other local official. Encourage him to make the awards and then sit down. When he is through, however, take care that he gets a good round of applause.

5. Musical Number.—By separating the two musical numbers in this fashion, you break up what might otherwise prove to be a long session of talk. Frequently efforts to achieve this end may prove a little difficult because one or the other of the musicians, if they are of the sort prevalent at banquets, will have to rush off at the earliest possible moment and visit a sick uncle in the country. At least that is the way it works out.

However, by exercising a little diplomacy, preferably enforced by a sledge hammer, you may be able to persuade one or the other of the two soloists to stay beyond the customary few minutes and thus separate the two musical numbers.

6. The Main Address.—The way the master of ceremonies handles the main address is the real test of his abilities.

The customary procedure in introducing the speaker is to tell a couple of anecdotes totally unrelated to the business in hand or to resurrect the story of the speaker's life and tell it in great detail. If it follows the usual pattern, the biographical sketch eventually works itself up to the grand climax in which the master of ceremonies in tremolant tones introduces the speaker as "my o-old fri-end!" He then proceeds to mispronounce the man's name as though he had heard it indistinctly only a moment or two before.

Needless to say, such a procedure is not likely to add a great deal to the spirit of the occasion.

Many people are afraid to ask the correct pronunciation of a name when they are about to make an introduction in public. They evidently feel that there is something embarrassing about having to ask for this information. Be assured, however, that it is much less embarrassing to ask in private than it is to blurt out the name in public and make a ludicrous mistake.

Not that the correct pronunciation of the speaker's name is all there is to it. Many masters of ceremonies are unnecessarily backward when it comes to digging out other facts about the speaker. They go beating about the bush, whispering here and whispering there, when the only proper source of information is the speaker himself. False modesty may prevent the speaker from telling you everything you ought to know, but if he has had any experience at all upon the public platform, he will supply you with enough facts to make an adequate introduction.

If, however, your speaker is the devil-may-care type or reluctant dragon who waves at you airily and chirps, "Oh, say anything you like! You can do it better than I can!", grab him firmly by the coat lapels and make him sit down until he gives you enough material to do a halfway decent job.

The main thing is to get your information at the earliest possible moment. By so doing, you will have more time in which to digest it and, as a result, make a greater success of your introduction.

When it comes to the introduction itself, give enough about

the speaker to make him sound interesting. Qualify him! Show, if possible, why he is especially fitted to discuss the subject in hand, whether it be the growing of petunias or the shearing of Rocky Mountain wild goats. Inject a little humor if you can. But remember: It is more important to get the speaker off to a good start than it is for the master of ceremonies to score himself.

After the speaker is through, thank him with dignity. Since the speaker is presumed to be an expert on the subject involved. Anything less would be an imposition.

7. The Installation.—It is customary, at most functions of the kind being described here, to present the installation before the speaker. Such a procedure is deadly and should be avoided. It is far better to have such formalities at the end, just before everyone is about to dash for the door. Otherwise the speaker labors under a very great handicap when he tries to give an address after what has been the climax of the evening.

Unless the ceremony is prescribed under Section 9a of the newly revised rules and bylaws, make it as brief as you can. Have a few words from the outgoing president. Have him or her hand a gavel or other symbolic instrument to the successor and let it go at that.

The new president may wish to say a word or two, but if he thinks this is the moment for an inaugural address, he is sadly mistaken. The effort now should be directed toward getting the program over as soon as possible.

When everything has been said, and all those present are sitting expectantly on the edges of their chairs, the master of ceremonies should thank all those present for their attendance, rap his gavel, and bring the meeting to an end. Do not delay after the last word has been spoken.

Advance Preparation

However, if things are to go as smoothly as indicated, a few pointers ought to be kept firmly in mind. After you have interviewed the chairman in charge of arrangements and have decided on the order of program as suggested earlier, make yourself a series of small cards or sheets of paper, each one headed with a section of the program as outlined above.

Previously, you were trying to decide on the order of the program. Now you are working on the individual parts.

Jot down on these cards the principal remarks which you wish to make about each event. Leave space at the bottom of the card so that you have room for additional material even as late as five seconds before you make the introduction. Make these notes as complete or as sketchy as you wish; but it is better to keep them brief. Otherwise you will spend most of your time between introductions pouring over your notes, and the top of your head looks singularly unattractive when displayed constantly to an audience.

Take extra blank cards or sheets of paper to the meeting with you, in the event that you have to make a complete change at the last moment because of the non-arrival of the speaker or some other catastrophe.

Make certain, likewise, that you have a pair of pencils with you. If you have only one pencil and it breaks you may have to spend several uncomfortable moments, whispering up one side of the table and down the other, before you discover someone with foresight enough to have brought an extra pencil with him.

As a matter of fact, you should keep a set of blank cards and an extra set of pencils in your good suit of clothes at all times. Then when you go off in that pre-banquet haze, you will be less likely to leave the tools of your trade at home.

Naturally the suggestions given above presuppose one thing: that you are going to do a little bit of advance preparatory work; that you are not going to wait until the last minute and then try to get the job done in a fury of head-scratching and perspiration.

Any method you adopt must be your own, but a good plan is to leave your notes lying on the dresser. Then when you tie your tie in the morning or fix your face, if you are a woman, you can jot down those brilliant little ideas that occurred to you during the night. During the day, when you are going about your regular business, you can dream up ideas and jot them down when you get home in the evening. Working in this fashion, you will get a fresher, more spontaneous style of introduction than if you try to do it all at one fell swoop. You will also find the work considerably easier.

The Fatal Moment

When you get to the dinner, look over the hall. Can you speak without shouting? If you are uncertain about being heard, have someone check to determine the exact tone of voice that it will be necessary for you to use.

If it happens that the tables are arranged in such a way that you cannot be seen by all of those present, do not hesitate to move to another part of the hall before the program begins. If this move proves impracticable and only a few are affected, give time at the start for those in an awkward position to move so they can see what is going on.

Check the lights. Chairmen at these affairs, especially if they are women, have a habit of turning off all the electricity and eating by candlelight. This is a great idea, but all of your carefully prepared notes will amount to nothing if you are unable to read them. Should it prove too dark, insist that a desk lamp and stand be provided, although the use of these accessories should be avoided if at all possible. They only stand between you and the audience. Check all of these things before the meeting begins, not afterwards.

Try, if possible, to circulate among those present, rather than hang back in a corner and bite your nails. Withdrawal leads to nervousness and a mounting tension and, besides, if you mingle with your audience before the meeting begins, you might accidentally pick up an idea or two that will prove useful to you in one of your introductions. Someone present may tell you a story or relate an incident that will enable you to localize one of your announcements and thus do a better job.

When at last you are seated at the table, try to carry on a running conversation with those beside you. Most head tables are as gloomy as a tomb, because the people sitting there concentrate upon the ordeal before them instead of trying to have a good time. All of them will do a better job—and so will you—if you concentrate instead on the spirit of the occasion. Some of your enjoyment may be communicated to the audience and, as a result, everyone will enjoy himself much more.

During the course of the dinner, people may come up to you with announcements which they imagine simply have to be made. Accommodate them if you can but, if the announcement seems trivial or inappropriate, suggest that they see the chairman in charge. If this suggestion proves impracticable and it looks as though the announcement will not fit into your carefully planned schedule, "forget" it.

Usually such announcements are brought to you by some ancient graybeard who imagines that the membership is just dying to know something that took place before the time of Columbus. You will have to use your own judgment when this happens to you, but you will find that dozens of these announcements can be forgotten conveniently without any loss to anyone. Of course, after the meeting is over, someone may needle you for having been so stupid as to forget, but it is usually easier and less embarrassing to make a profuse apology than it is to make a senseless announcement.

When the time comes to begin, do so immediately. Do not delay, but start at the earliest possible moment. A good time is the instant before the last waitress disappears through the door with the last pitcher of cream. In certain circumstances, it may be necessary to hurry the waitress.

If there is any doubt, it is a good idea to check and see to it that arrangements are being made to clear the tables promptly. Professionals in a hotel will almost always get out of your way as quickly as possible. The Ladies' Aid in Pumpkin Junction may need a little urging.

Do not dally either because everyone seems to be having

a good time. Someone is sure to make this suggestion if the audience is chattering a good deal. Do not do it! The audience may not be having such a wonderful time later on in the evening, if the program runs too long and the time to avert that is at the beginning. The success of the luncheon clubs has been predicated upon a fast beginning and a quick end. Get the attention of those present and start with forthrightness and courage.

As the evening progresses, additional ideas may occur to you which seem suitable for use in this or that section of the entertainment. Use them if you can, but it pays to be very careful in this regard. Some of these ideas, thought up under the stress of the occasion, may prove to be a little strained. Do not use such ideas unless you are absolutely certain of their effect. Some very embarrassing blunders have been committed by toastmasters who have indulged in these last-minute inspirations, and jokes which sound exceedingly funny before they are uttered have the most lamentable way of back-firing and blowing right up in their perpetrator's face. In the beginning, at least, it is wiser to stick to your carefully laid plan than it is to wander off on untried pathways and have a disaster.

Relax if you can, but if this proves impossible, at least try to listen to the rest of the speakers on the program. It will help keep your mind off your own thoughts. And who knows? You might even accidentally learn something.

Sample Introductions

The following is an example of how the dinner described in the text might be handled by a master of ceremonies. Although purely imaginary, the sample is more typical than you might think.

Ladies and gentlemen, good evening! I am your master of ceremonies. Perhaps you do not know who I am. You have nothing on me. There are times when I scarcely know myself. At other times, I'm glad I am a stranger to myself, especially in the morning when I get a good look at myself in the mirror when shaving. On such occasions, I have often wished I was someone else.

Nevertheless, I do feel that you should know who I am. You look, most of you, as though you had seen considerable of this world, and I'm sure you'll be able to survive the shock. I am Waldo Waldenheimer. I'm a lawyer here in East Fudnuk, and I know as many stories about lawyers as you do, but I'm not going to tell them now.

As a matter of fact, since I am a lawyer and not previously acquainted with your program, I was doubly impressed with what you people have accomplished. That fact, I think, will be made amply evident later in the evening when recognition will be given for some of the outstanding work done during the year and new officers will be installed.

This is one of the reasons why I am especially glad to be here this evening. The other, of course, is that I get a free meal.

On behalf of the committee in charge, I welcome you to this annual banquet of the Society of Petunia Growers and hope that you will have a pleasant and entertaining evening.

As part of that entertainment, we are fortunate in being able to present a pair of students from the local high school. One of these is Dolores Doddles. She has been a pupil of Maestro Facetti for a number of years and is a specialist on the trombone. Although only fifteen years old, Miss Doddles told me before the program began that she took up the trombone because it is the only instrument on which you can get anywhere by letting things slide. Miss Doddles will now play an arrangement for the trombone of "Pastorale," by Ignace Sweitz.

Music. After the number, the master of ceremonies leads the applause.

Thank you, Miss Doddles, for your contribution to this evening's program.

At this point in the proceedings, I was scheduled to give a brief lecture on "How to be a Flying Saucer" but, because of the press of other activities, I have decided to restrict myself to a few necessary announcements.

First, I have been asked to thank those who have contributed in any way to the success of this event. These include especially the members of the committee who functioned so ably under the leadership of Hyman Hausner. There was some doubt, at first, over whether Hyman would be able to arrange anything so complicated as a banquet, but at least none of us were worried about Hyman. It was his wife. She saw him boil water at home once and has been a little uncertain about him ever since.

Nevertheless since things have gone off so well and we are indebted to Mr. Hausner and his helpers for an excellent meal, I suggest that we give a great big hand to the ladies and gentlemen on the committee of arrangements.

The master of ceremonies leads a round of applause for the chairman and his helpers.

The committee in charge, however, is not the only group of people to be honored here tonight. As in the past, members of your society are to be honored for distinguished achievement throughout the year.

To present these honors, we have with us this evening a very special guest. He is Herman Humplemyer, proprietor of Humplemyer's Greenhouse. We are very grateful to Mr. Humplemyer for being willing to take time from his professional duties this evening and bother with us—a group of amateurs. Ordinarily, too, Mr. Humplemyer would prefer to say it with flowers, but tonight he is content to stick to words. Mr. Humplemyer.

The master of ceremonies leads a round of applause as Humplemyer rises to make the awards and another round at the end of the ceremony.

Thank you, Mr. Humplemyer, for your services this evening. Our thanks must be expressed in words because we know that you already have enough bouquets of your own.

Earlier we were treated to a trombone solo by one of the gifted pupils of Maestro Facetti of the local high school. In preparing these young people for their work in the high school orchestra, Maestro Facetti has not neglected the French horn as well. Now there is very little I can tell you about this instrument except that it looks like an explosion in a spaghetti factory and is very difficult to play. However, in the hands of Doris Fudd, who will play an arrangement from the works of Bach, the French horn will speak equally well in all languages. Miss Fudd.

Music. After the number, the master of ceremonies sees to it that the young lady gets an adequate hand.

Thank you, Miss Fudd. We are very grateful to you and Miss Doddles for your willingness to appear here this evening. Thank you very much. After listening to you, we know why it is that our high school music department is rated so highly.

In fact we are indebted to our educational institutions this evening in more ways than one. Our principal speaker is from the State Agricultural College at West Bend. I don't believe that any of us who pretend to the slightest acquaintanceship with horticulture are unfamiliar with the name of our speaker. He has been a professor at State College for over fifteen years. In that time, he has developed any number of new flowers, and tonight he comes to us after having just recently

been honored by the Petunia Society of Europe. It was he who developed
the petunia known as "Oslo Glory." I am sure that we are all happy
to welcome him here this evening and we await with pleasure his
words on a very important subject, "Do Petunias Have a Place in
Foreign Affairs?" I now present Professor Oliver Ageratum of the
State College at West Bend. Professor Ageratum.

The Professor rises as the master of ceremonies starts the
applause. At the conclusion, the master of ceremonies again
leads the applause.

Thank you, Professor. On behalf of the society, our thanks for a
very interesting and educational talk. Judging from the rapt attention
which you received, I am sure that everyone here appreciates very
much what you had to say.

We have one final rite to perform on our program this evening. As
most of you know, the growing season is none too long. In fact in these
latitudes it is rather short. We barely get time to keep down the weeds.

Now in this organization there is a group of people who have been
growing for a full year. They started out rather slowly, then burst into
glorious bloom.

Naturally we're referring to the officers of this society. I think
you'll agree that they have been exceptionally sturdy bloomers and, to
use a common expression, our garden has been a riot of color this year.
However, all good things must come to an end, and I'm afraid, if these
plants are left out in the cold much longer, they may get nipped by
an early frost. To avoid that possibility, we are about to install new
officers who will serve as the heads of this organization for the coming
year. As installing officer, I am happy to present Mr. Gerald Snifter,
an old and valued member of our society, who will perform this important function. Mr. Snifter.

The master of ceremonies may do as suggested in the foregoing, or he may introduce the old and the new officers himself. In either event, speeches during this period should be
kept at a minimum.

Thank you, Mr. Snifter. Now, on behalf of the committee in charge,
I wish to thank you all for your attendance here this evening. It has
been most heartening, and I'm sure that we all can look forward to
another year of growth and development under the new officers.

The master of ceremonies raps the gavel.

We stand adjourned.

CHAPTER TWO

ROUTINING A PROGRAM

To be quite frank about it, there are very few rules which, if followed, can help you to do a good job of routining a program. The entire field is somewhat like playing the piano by ear. If you have a good musical sense, the melody may be pleasing. If not, the results may be too horrible to contemplate.

In many cases, you will not have to routine the program; it will be done for you. But as master of ceremonies, responsible in large measure for its final success, you should at least retain the semblance of a veto over any arrangement of the program which does not suit you. Otherwise you may be faced with trying to sell a product which, by its very nature, is doomed to failure.

You may be told that the order of the program cannot be changed. Someone must catch a train, or the arrangement was made by Mrs. Elmira Fudnuk, the well-known horse lover and society matron. It is therefore sacrosanct. Nothing, absolutely nothing can be done!

When that happens, you are faced with either one of two choices: Either the program must be changed or you suggest politely that someone else be delegated to handle the affair. After all, you, as well as Mrs. Fudnuk, have your reputation to maintain and, as for the person catching the train, it almost invariably happens that he is never in such a hurry as at first advertised. The skillful speaker, with plenty of experience, rarely accepts an engagement unless he is able to fulfill it properly. It is the inexperienced speaker who is most likely to behave like a prima donna and demand all sorts of extra consideration.

Usually when it appears that a previously arranged program is going to be difficult to handle, a few tactful words to the right people will work wonders. Should the program fail, you as master of ceremonies will receive a substantial portion of the blame. Therefore, it pays to be firm. Sometimes compromises will have to be made. A speaker may be unavoidably delayed. There may be illness or last-minute changes, in which case you will have to give and take. But a master of ceremonies will generally do better in a program arrangement with which he feels thoroughly comfortable.

A Definition

However, before you consider this phase of your work, it might be well to indulge in one definition. "Routining a program" is arranging the various parts in such a way that they have maximum effect. It takes into account such phases of the work as a proper opening, coherence, progression, contrast, climax, and a number of mechanical factors which must also be considered.

Lest the subject of routining sound too complicated, remember that no one knows very much about it. The subject is one of the black arts. However badly you do it the first time, you will never quite match the mistakes already made by those who are supposed to know something about the business. So don't worry! There are rules, but the tremendous diversity of material available makes it almost impossible to formulate a simple set which will do you any good.

A Few Examples

The best way to learn routining is through studying some of the more successful examples around you. They are everywhere, and you will be surprised at how quickly the principles of program planning become evident if you know for what you are seeking.

Take a good look at the neighborhood moving picture. Probably the program begins with a news reel—a bridge or transition from the world outside to the entertainment which lies ahead. Following this, there are the trailers—previews of later attractions which, in a sense, are news items, too, because they inform the patrons of coming events. A comedy is next.

Then while the audience is presumed to be in its most malleable state, the designing manager creeps upon them with the commercial advertisements. After that and at long last comes the feature picture, the climax for which the audience presumably paid money.

Listen to one of your favorite radio programs. After the introduction, the comedian appears first. He tells a string of jokes calculated to establish him in the minds of the audience as the star of the show. Then comes a commercial. After the commercial, the orchestra plays a selection. During the dialogue which follows, the guest star is introduced. The second commercial is presented next. The orchestra plays another number which, for variety's sake, may also feature a vocal solo by some well-known singer. At the end, the guest star and the comedian launch into the playlet or skit which has been designed as the climax of the program. There is a very definite sense of progression as the program moves along—a skillful blending of the various elements into a cohesive whole.

Examine a few of those long-playing records which are made up of a number of short, individual selections on each side. See how, in the arrangement of music, identical principles of program planning are followed. One side begins with a bright, cheerful number; a waltz is next; a tango or rhumba may be the third number heard while the side concludes with a novelty.

On a somewhat different scale, much the same thing was done with the program outlined in the first chapter. An effort was made to combine the various elements in such a way as to bring out the best in each or, to be quite frank about it, to make them seem better than they actually were.

An operation of this type is called showmanship, and there is nothing dishonest about it. Showmanship is perfectly legitimate, provided you make no effort to deceive. Your audience will expect a certain effort to gild the lily and will be disappointed if it is not forthcoming. Therefore, you are duty bound to make every number on the program seem as good as you possibly can.

You may never supervise a recording session, routine a neighborhood movie, or appear on a national broadcast. But the foregoing suggestions kept in mind, will help you to do a better job, regardless of the type of program you have to handle.

The Opening

A good opening belongs at the beginning. Probably, it sounds ridiculous to make such a statement, but you would be surprised at how many times it gets buried near the end.

Go back to the first chapter, where the petunia growers were meeting. If you wait until just before the installation to remind the audience that this is the annual meeting where such things are expected to take place, you may be heading for trouble. You are nearing the end of your program. The audience is weary and, if you take time for such trivia now, they may decide to yawn in your face, figuratively, if not literally.

Your opening is designed to catch the attention of the audience and make them understand what is to follow. Most audiences are fairly co-operative and, if you make the slightest effort to provide an interesting opening, you will be rewarded out of all proportion to the amount of labor involved.

There are really only two ways to catch the attention of any audience. One is by surprise, and the other is the slower, more insidiously developed transition from one situation to another. Surprise may be present in the latter, but it is not the principal ingredient.

Each method has its advantages and disadvantages, and if you are wise you will try and discover which system is best adapted to your own personality and to the special problem you have in hand. The method of surprise has its value. It wakes up your audience. Its disadvantage lies in the fact that you have to pile on more surprises if you are going to keep them awake. With the slower method, you run the risk of never getting your audience awake at all, but it does have the advantage of giving you something on which to build over the long haul.

For instance, you are scheduled to be master of ceremonies at the annual clambake of the Allied Poetasters of America. Before the program begins, the Poetasters present have been regaled with the indigestible collation which passes as food on such occasions. They are in a state of semi-coma. If you shoot off a Roman candle to gain their attention, you are apt to create, instead of good will, a condition of slow burning resentment which will do you no good. In place of being forced to build from the Roman candle, it is better to take these people gently by the hand and lead them slowly in the way you wish them to go.

On the one hand, if the audience is small, use a more casual method of making an approach. If, on the other hand, you are faced with the problem of presenting a huge spectacle in front of a large outdoor amphitheater, you must begin with something guaranteed to catch the attention of an audience that size.

However, such things need only be relative. It is not necessary to give it everything you have in order to gain the attention of an audience at the start of a program. In fact, you cannot afford to make the effort. Some room must be left for expansion later and, besides, if you begin too loudly or with too much gusto, you run the risk of antagonizing your audience. By projecting yourself into the situation slowly, you can feel out your audience at the beginning and thus stand a better chance of gaining their sympathetic attention as the program proceeds.

Here is an example. You are the master of ceremonies at a February sales meeting of the Ice-Cap Refrigerator Company. A new line of refrigerators is to be introduced. It is your job to transport your listeners from the snowy scene outside to the time next June when the new refrigerators finally go on sale. Your opening might sound like this:

Gentlemen: It's not always easy to look ahead. Today, however, we can enjoy it. We can look forward to a time next June when storms such as we are experiencing today are a thing of the past. We can then examine the spring flowers and say to ourselves that a day like today never really happened. We can also look forward to the time when the new Ice-Cap refrigerators, etc., etc.

Such an introduction takes cognizance of the present situation of the audience and transports them pleasantly to the time when action will be demanded.

The Climax

While you are arranging a program as suggested in the first chapter, it seems fairly certain that you will have no difficulty in deciding what is to be the main event of the evening. It is the principal speech, the principal performance or the principal person. It may be the sole reason for the existence of the entire program. If, however, it seems that you are faced with handling a program which has no natural climax, you will have to invent one.

Sometimes when you are looking over the singularly uninspired material which you are expected to introduce, you will find a piece of entertainment that seems relatively neglected, that is fresh and new or otherwise unusual. You may have sufficient inventiveness to take that particular number out of context and build it into the climax of the evening, although admittedly the possibilities in this regard are frequently limited.

In other instances, it may be possible to build a climax by combining features, as with the accordion recital that winds up with all the performers playing at once, after a program that consisted mainly of accordion solos.

Given a program that simply drizzles along and gets nowhere, you may have little choice but to get it over with as rapidly as possible; although here again everything is relative. If your closing is only a little bigger or better than your opening, you may be able to persuade your audience that you have presented a suitable climax without anyone's being any the wiser.

Progression

If you are arranging a rather extensive program, the big problem is to handle those parts that lie in between the opening and the closing. Here you may experience a little difficulty because, in the movement of a program from one part to the next, something should happen besides the passage of time. The audience should be made to feel that something worth while is going on, that there is a definite stage of development between one act and the next, or that something is being added either to their enjoyment or to the fund of knowledge which they possess.

In this connection, it is well to remember that acts and people have a specific gravity. It cannot be measured except in the probable reaction of the audience to what is presented, but it is important. It may not have anything at all to do with the merit of the act itself or your own personal reaction to it, but, if your audience demands one act as the climax of the program, it will have to be presented that way, or both you and the audience are going to be very unhappy.

Another illustration may suffice. In a symposium on the Missouri Valley Authority, one speaker gave the geological background of the Missouri River, a second spoke on its present-day development, while a third outlined the organizational setup planned under the proposed Authority.

In following such an outline, the audience was taken by logical steps toward the desired end of the program, which was some sort of decision about the Missouri Valley Authority.

It would have been ridiculous, for instance, to have given the geological story at the conclusion of the program, because its import is essential to an understanding of the other two parts. Psychologically speaking, it would have been wrong, too, because it is in the third or final stage, the one that tells about the plans for the proposed Authority, that a basis for future judgment is given. This is progression.

What the word means in a general way is that the bigger, more colorful or impressive acts should come near the end.

Or if you are stimulating your audience to action, such as taking a stand on the Missouri Valley Authority mentioned in the previous example, that part of the program which demands action, such as a vote one way or the other, should come somewhere near the point where the action is taken. In other words, when the purpose of the meeting is to pass a resolution or register an opinion, everything that happens at the meeting must progress to the point where this step is taken. Anything after that is an anti-climax.

If you have attended many concerts, you will note that the heavier, more complex pieces come near the beginning, when the audience is presumed to be comparatively fresh. Lighter music by modern composers is heard near the end. The general idea is to send the audience home in a happy frame of mind and, at the same time, preserve some sort of chronological sequence in the presentation of the music. That, too, is a form of progression. It would not do, after bellowing a popular ditty, to launch into a dolorous lament by some hardy ancient long dead before the time of Bach.

Contrast

When you are trying to organize the various elements that go into the make-up of a program, you will soon discover that there is another important factor which must be taken into consideration. That factor is contrast. A Viennese waltz followed by a tune in Latin tempo provides contrast in rhythm, phrasing, and musical color.

In the terminology of show business, this factor—contrast—is also known as change of pace. After something fast, offer something slow; after seriousness, offer comedy; after music, offer talk; and after the grotesque, offer something in the sentimental mood. In so doing, you avoid a petrifying sameness that will rapidly put your audience to sleep.

However, it should be borne in mind that contrast, too, is relative. In a program of cornet solos, a single number on the vibraphone provides a lot of contrast.

Oftentimes it is only necessary to achieve contrast within a particularly narrow range. It is not necessary to drag something in by the heels merely to achieve contrast. A shock treatment is not required. Frequently only a little contrast is required, but it should be present.

Should everything else fail, a certain amount of contrast can be achieved through varying the manner in which the act is presented. Should the program, for instance, be a recital by a succession of young lady pianists, some distinction in the numbers can be obtained by having each girl appear in a different colored dress, although here admittedly such a distinction is merely superficial. True contrast should be obtained through having variety in the music, which is the basic material of the program. A change in presentation, however, certainly makes it easier for everyone.

Contrast also can be obtained by changing the physical position from which the act performs. If you have a musical program before the speeches at a banquet, for instance, try to have the music presented from a different section of the hall. It eases the eyes and the audience will not so quickly become bored by having to stare at the same dull old end of the room.

Some of these things may sound trivial, and they probably are, but if you are faced with a program that seems to be dying on its feet, it may be worth while to remember them and use them occasionally.

If contrast cannot be obtained in any other way, vary your introductions, making one serious, another humorous. If you work hard enough, you may be able to disguise the fact that the whole program is as dull as dishwater.

Coherence

As has been intimated while hammering away on the subject of contrast, it is not a good idea to carry the practice too far. On a program featuring Harry Nimblefingers, the internationally renowned concert pianist, it is not necessary to present a few peurile peeps from Percival Periwinkle, the amateur flutist, merely to provide a little contrast.

When changing from one act to another, try to do it in such a way that there is no danger of shocking the sensibilities of your audience. That brings up another question. Many times, because of what takes place, you will be inclined to doubt that your audience has any sensibilities. If this lack is genuine, however, you are obligated to try to develop some sensibilities. You cannot escape your responsibilities, either way you look at it.

Many times when you are introducing a program, you will discover numbers which are there only by virtue of the fact that their perpetrators are related by marriage to someone with a good deal of money or because such perpetrator is the friend of a friend of a friend.

If you become aware of such a situation early enough in the preliminary stages of the planning, you can often ease the offender out by showing that such an act, through being totally unrelated to what goes on before or after, will only suffer in consequence. A few words, discreetly applied, can be a kindness. At the same time, such an excision can cause plenty of trouble. If it looks as though you cannot get rid of the jarring note without throwing a tantrum, it may be best to ignore the dictates of your artistic conscience and announce the act as if it were the greatest thing of its kind in the world. Do not be surprised, though, if someone connected with the offending piece of merchandise comes to you afterwards and blames you for the fact that it was a failure. That is the way things are in this world. You will simply have to make the best of it.

With skill, a master of ceremonies can bridge a broad distance between various types of presentations, but he cannot be expected to perform a miracle.

Mechanical Problems

The points which have been discussed thus far are intangible factors which float somewhere between here and the great beyond. But they are by no means all of the problems which have to be considered when hacking together a program.

On the stage there are mechanical exigencies which have to be taken into account. Acrobats have to erect a long pole on which they balance each other. Magicians have to stuff rabbits into their hats. The piano must be moved from one side of the stage to the other in order to accommodate the girl singer who looks well only from one half of her face.

Customarily, when you are working with amateurs, they will forget to tell you these things. The committee in charge will know nothing about them. All concerned will conspire to keep you in utter and complete ignorance. Then when you announce the act, expecting it to begin immediately, you discover to your horror that nothing happens. You will be left high and dry in the center of the stage, while the act waits in the wings, grimacing, to the accompaniment of weird and wonderful gestures meaning precisely nothing. Finally to keep things from going to pieces altogether, you yourself rush forth with the missing piece of equipment, or you commit suicide in full view of the audience to keep them entertained.

If you even suspect that an upcoming act has equipment which must be placed during an interval, check beforehand. Find out how long it takes to place the equipment and then, in front of the curtain or in another part of the hall or in a spotlight while the rest of the stage remains in darkness, fill the interval by regaling the audience with stories designed to keep them in a happy frame of mind.

At the same time it does no harm to impress upon the act the necessity for exercising due haste while getting their equipment upon the stage. Most of them will co-operate. Also the master of ceremonies has the right to insist upon a reasonable degree of silence during the operation. If you are expected to hold the stage alone, while those behind you set their equipment, the least they can do is keep it slightly more quiet than a foundry.

You are now asking yourself, "What has all this to do with

routining a program?" The answer is plain. If you have a mechanical problem, if equipment must be placed, you will have to arrange your program in such a way that it can be done without interrupting the smooth flow of the entertainment. It will have to be done regardless of any considerations for coherence, progression, or anything else. All of which shows what happens to artistic principles when practical problems are involved.

CHAPTER THREE

ORIGINAL INTRODUCTIONS

When working out an original introduction, you have to think of the basic elements that go into its make-up. They are the elements of which you have heard before: your old friends of the newspaper world—who, what, why, when, and where. Who is going to give this talk? What is he going to talk about? Where is he from? Why is it important that I listen to him now? Answer all of these questions in any introduction, and you are not going to stray very far from the point. The problem is to do it in such a manner that your contribution to the program is both interesting and entertaining. If you are to achieve that end, however, you should understand what you are trying to accomplish.

An introduction is like a bridge. It spans the distance between two points. Better yet, it spans the distance between one state of mind on the part of your audience and another.

If you are making an opening introduction, its spans the distance between the state of mind enjoyed by the audience before the start of the program and the one they ought to have to appreciate the first number. Thereafter, in successive stages, you lead your audience, point by point, through the various states of mind needed to appreciate the different parts of the program. At the end, when the program is all over, anything you say is designed to send the audience home feeling that they had a good time or that the occasion, at the very least, was worthwhile.

With this definition, it is now possible to go ahead and dream up something that might be used in actual introduction.

A Sample Introduction

Suppose you are a county agent. The East Conundrum Homemakers' Club is holding a meeting, and it is a part of your job to introduce a talk by Elmer Fudnuk, the well-known poultry raiser and chicken fancier.

That being true, it might be well to go back to those five W's and see how it is that the interests of Mr. Fudnuk fit in with those of the Homemakers' Club. In the first place, who is Mr. Fudnuk? Why is it important that the homemaker's club listen to him? What is he going to talk about? It is by thinking through the answers to questions like these that you arrive at the material which must be present in your announcement.

Mr. Fudnuk is a well-known poultry breeder. But what proof is there of his eminence? If he has recently received some recognition that makes it seem more important than ever for the Homemakers to listen to him, that information should be included in the announcement. The more recent the information the better. Its recency proves that Mr. Fudnuk has not gone to seed and is now resting on his past glories.

Is the subject on which he is speaking of immediate interest to the Homemakers' Club? Should it be? By showing its importance and by relating it to the immediate interests of the audience, you can heighten interest in the prospective peroration of Mr. Fudnuk. By finding the answers to all of these questions and by answering all of the questions that might logically be asked by the audience, you perform your primary function as a master of ceremonies.

Of course, there is a little more to it than that. You have to provide some pleasure as well.

A simple and straightforward announcement might go as follows: "Thank you, Mrs. Hotchkiss, for your talk on 'Home Canning Can Be Fun.' We will now hear an address by Elmer Fudnuk, the well-known butter-and-egg man, on the subject, 'Why Do Hens Lay Oval Eggs Instead of Round Ones?' "

An introduction like the foregoing accomplishes the purpose. It gets you there, but it gives you no enjoyment along the way. It is like breezing through a scenic wonderland at a hundred miles an hour without a guide to point out the features of interest. There is no fun in it, as there should be. Besides giving your audience the simple facts, you are expected to provide a little entertainment, too.

Take the sample above, dress it up a bit, and see how it comes out.

> Thank you, Mrs. Hotchkiss, for the information you have given us. After listening to you, we can understand that "Can it!" is no longer just a slang expression. We are very grateful to you for taking the time to come and give us the benefit of your experience.
>
> Naturally there are other subjects which are also interesting and worth while. But I want you to know that the next one has had me baffled for some time. Modern science has wrestled with the problem but seems able to devise nothing that can change the present outlook. I refer to the shape of eggs. They are usually oval. Why? Why shouldn't they be round or square or any other shape that pleases the aesthetic sensibilities of those who have to eat them? Was the shape of eggs decided by all the hens acting in concert, as a sort of union agreement, or is it simply a habit too difficult to break?
>
> To discuss this titillating subject, we are happy to have with us Mr. Elmer Fudnuk, the well-known poultry breeder and judge of eggs. Mr. Fudnuk had the prize-winning rooster at last year's fair, but the rooster, we are assured, did not lay the egg, regardless of shape or size. Neither will Mr. Fudnuk.
>
> I know that we are all happy to hear a discussion of this momentous subject. Mr. Fudnuk.

The master of ceremonies then sits down, after leading a round of applause for the rising speaker.

An example, such as the one given, is facetious, but it illustrates a number of very important points. It does not go directly into the business at hand without adding a little "plus value" along the way. The bare bones of the skeleton are hidden underneath the art of the introduction.

While building the situation for the next speaker, the master of ceremonies injects an element of mystery. Suspense is created. The audience is led to believe that the talk might be serious; the reference to science accomplishes that. Then when the laughter comes, the amount is greater because surprise is present also. Each step not only gives an additional fact about the speaker or his subject but presents it entertainingly as well.

That is really all there is to it, regardless of whether you are introducing one man or a chorus, a debate or a comic monologue, a German band or a full symphony. By taking all of these factors into account or, at least, as many of them as you can, you seek to give the audience all the information they require and, at the same time, keep them entertained.

Two Good Ideas

In your search for fresh material, there are two sources which should not be neglected. One is the act or the person being introduced. Often the speakers you introduce have had a great deal of experience before the public. Long before you reach the scene, other masters of ceremonies may have introduced them in a singularly effective way. You can do no better than to follow suit. Talk to the person involved. Find out what was said on previous occasions. If it fits your style, use it. It will save you a lot of trouble, and, besides, someone else is almost certain to use your ideas if they are good.

There is a kind of pool—a bank from which you are permitted to draw if you make a contribution of your own from time to time. For instance, in the case of the act which achieved an especially effective introduction by some master of ceremonies, that introduction, in a sense, was contributed to the act. You can use it, provided you do not object when some other master of ceremonies uses your material in a similar way.

Material that is closely identified with another master of ceremonies, however, should not be used. That belongs to him. The ethical use of such material consists in deciding whether or not it belongs in the public domain.

If it has been used so much that everyone knows it, then it is in the public domain, and you may use it, too. If it belongs to the act or the speaker, you may use it when you introduce that act or that speaker. If, however, it belongs to another master of ceremonies, you are cheating if you try to use it.

In the process of improving your introductions, naturally you do not go up to a speaker and ask him how it was done in some other town. You merely ask if there is any special way in which he would like to be introduced. He will then volunteer the information about how some other master of ceremonies made the introduction if he thinks it might prove helpful. You will then decide whether or not you want to use the information he has given you.

Another method of getting greater freshness and appeal into your work lies through conversations with key persons who may be members of your audience. Choose a not-too-old old-timer—some person who has been a long-time member of the group or organization before which you are scheduled to appear. Choose one who is not so senile that he dwells in the past instead of the present or future. Talk to him casually. Invariably such a pump, if properly primed, will pour forth a world of information about the people you are going to address, their hopes, their fears, and their aspirations. By tying these into your introductions, not obviously but with humor and understanding, you can gain an effect obtainable in no other way. You establish an intimacy with your audience that pays off in both laughter and applause.

Using a Theme

One way of getting originality into your introductions is through the use of a theme.

At a football dinner, for instance, it is possible to spice your introductions by using football terms out of context. For example: "He's one of the fanciest broken field runners we have seen in some time—in the field of the fiddle solo!"

The only trouble with such a solution lies in knowing when to stop. Sooner or later you are going to find a number which is too good to throw away and yet it does not fit your theme. Rather than jeopardize the number, forget the theme for the moment and go on with a straight introduction or at least one more appropriate to the subject.

When using a theme, do not beat it to death. After all, it is only spice and too much of it may spoil the entire cake. One lady used flowers as her theme. She compared each number to a different kind of flower. She labored the point so heavily that, before she was through, no one present would have sent a bouquet to his own mother's funeral.

Clichés

Avoid clichés. In working out your own original introductions, avoid words or phrases which are so overworked that they have little meaning.

It will not do, for instance, to say, "Without further ado, I now give you Elmer Fudnuk!"

Who cares whether you create any ado or not, least of all, the audience? You can create all the ado you want, as long as you make it interesting. That is why you are there. To be quite blunt about it, the master of ceremonies who uses such a word is apologizing. He feels in his heart of hearts, that he is creating an ado—senseless noise—and that is generally what he is doing if he had to lean on the phrase. You do not "give" anyone, either, especially if the speaker is more important than you are. You "present" him.

Another cliché which should be avoided is the phrase, "in his own right." A man is an artist or musician "in his own right." You can sit for hours and try to figure out what this phrase means. Yet it is constantly being used when presenting those whose fields of endeavor are a little bit out of the ordinary. It adds nothing to the occasion and, like the word above, is, in a sense, an apology for the person presented.

One of the most original ways of making an introduction is to stand straight up on your own feet and say what you have to say forthrightly and without apology to anyone. Your audience may be so amazed that there will be no time to discover that what you had to say was not especially original.

Watch, too, for those clichés which seem to go the rounds periodically. They are not hard to recognize. Everyone will be using them, and they will be heard all of the time on radio or television. All singers will be "honey-voiced." All businessmen will be "red-blooded," or all orchestra leaders will be "genial." Avoid them when you can.

Whenever you use a word or phrase which has been bandied

about until it has lost all meaning, your audience will think of the last time they heard it, instead of what you are trying to say.

Avoid also those hardy perennials "It gives me great pleasure to present" or "I am now happy to present." You can lead up to the final words of your introduction of a speaker in a dozen different ways, if you are careful to give the problem a moment's thought.

For instance, take the case of the master of ceremonies who is to introduce a speaker who is scheduled to talk on the subject of atomic energy. In place of going through the routine above, say, "I am certain that we all can profit by what our speaker will have to say on this most important subject. Professor Snodgrass." By handling the subject in this way, by refusing to follow the pattern that has been established, you add a freshness to your work that redounds to the credit of both you and the speaker.

Selling the Article

In working out your own introductions, there is one point which is almost more important than anything else you have to remember. Whether you are presenting a program of pure entertainment or something more serious, you are charged with a certain degree of responsibility in taking care that what you have to offer is properly sold. To the average person, this means lauding it to the skies. Nothing, however, is further from the truth. It will not do to present an act as sensational when it is nothing of the sort.

Such a method does not work because it is basically untrue. Unless the act you are presenting has done everything you say it has, unless it has appeared before the crowned heads of Europe, on a New York television show, or in Uncle Charlie's Old-Time Minstrels, it will not do to say so. The average audience today is far too sophisticated to accept any such hokum.

Your job is to detect the saleable angle in any commodity

you have to offer and then present it in such a way that your audience "buys" what you have to sell.

Doing the job properly also requires that you know something about audiences. So the next question arises: What do audiences like to buy? The answer is that they will buy almost anything that is properly presented and that has some merit of its own.

Audiences will accept a well-known concert violinist with perfect technique and a reputation extending round the globe. The same audiences, under proper conditions, will also accept the performance of a six-year-old boy who can only play the instrument with a fair degree of facility.

The difference lies in the level at which the audience and the entertainment meet. If the performer is one of accepted technique and accomplishment, the level can be high. If not, no effort should be made to lead the audience to expect anything other than what is going to be presented. In other words, a basic honesty must be present.

But how do you detect those parts of an act or presentation which are most acceptable to an audience? Ten thousand examples could be given, and none of them would be worth a nickel unless you understand that there is also another quality which figures prominently in the success of your work. That quality is sympathy. You must be sympathetic toward what your audience expects of you or you will not be able to do the best job possible.

To repeat the example given earlier, if you are introducing the child violinist, it would not do to present him as a child prodigy unless he were generally recognized as such, and even then the wisdom of such a course would be doubtful. The audience would detect instantly an attempt to exploit the talents of the child and would rightfully resent it.

If, however, you explain that here is a little boy who has studied the violin for only eight months and who, at the age of six, shows exceptional promise, you are placing the picture in the proper frame, and the audience knows what to expect.

Without question, some of them may think he should be at home sucking a lollipop, but you will have discharged your responsibility.

Actually, what you must do is dwell upon a single facet of the act or the personality involved. With the child violinist, you seek to sell his ability to play the instrument at such a tender age. With a magician, you stress his ability to perform card tricks with uncanny skill or, with a speaker, you stress his special qualifications for handling the subject involved.

In selling, such a process is known as pressing the hot button, and it works as well in selling entertainment as it does in selling shoes or anything else. No one buys shoes, however, because of the personality of the salesman. Shoes are bought because the buyer needs them or expects to get a certain amount of pleasure out of a second pair. It is a matter of self-interest. When selling something to an audience, you will accomplish much more if you base at least a part of your appeal on self-interest. Answer the question, "What is there in this for me?"

An appeal to self-interest is not so important when you are presenting a juggler or a pair of trained dogs. But when you are appearing before a banquet audience, and the speaker is scheduled to talk on a fairly serious subject such as taxes or the state of the nation, both you and the audience are going to get along much better if at least part of your appeal is based on self-interest. You show them that it is to their interest to listen to the subject under discussion. You explain why it is important for them to listen to a talk on these particular subjects.

The matter of self-interest applies even to the juggler and the dogs. The audience will be far more inclined to watch either one or the other if they can be convinced beforehand that the performance will be worth their while. Even the desire to be entertained is part of a person's feeling of self-interest.

Through appealing to the audience at their own level, you will get much further than if you base your approach on something located nebulously between the now and the great hereafter. Try always to relate what you are doing to the needs and desires of your audience.

The Final Stage

Given these suggestions for devising original introductions, it should not be too difficult to get your material properly organized for presentation before an audience.

Three-by-five-inch cards are ideal for the purpose; but, as suggested earlier, do not write more than key words or phrases on these cards. They serve only as reminders. Neither does it look well to hold the cards in your hands, unless you have to quote facts and figures which are difficult to remember. Even then you should make an effort to get along without the cards.

Do not write out your announcements, either to read or to quote from memory. Such procedure may be necessary in radio broadcasting, because of the time element. But on all other occasions you should speak to your audience extemporaneously and with as few notes as possible. When reading, you lose contact with your audience by having to keep your eyes glued to the card. If you memorize, you have to stick to an exact arrangement of your material when, for best effect, it might be necessary to change your approach at the last moment because of changed circumstances.

Practice announcements if you wish, but do not go over them until they are stale and pointless. Too much practice with extemporaneous announcements is bad because, when you get in front of the audience, you are inclined to remember what you said at practice instead of concentrating on your audience, which is what you should do. Memorize ideas, but leave the words flexible, so you can change them to meet the varying moods of your audience or to meet changing conditions.

If you must practice, do it on something else, e. g., material that may not be used before an audience. Practice extemporaneous delivery by having a friend work out a series of flash cards—pictures cut from advertisements, pictures which tell a story. Have him flash the cards before you while you give a play-by-play description of what you see, in the manner of a radio announcer. You will be surprised at what a little work along this line can do for you.

Naturally if you are going to present the same material over and over again or continue to introduce the same program, you can memorize your announcements and give them with slight variations as the occasion demands.

Of necessity, however, much of your work will be impromptu. What you really need is a command of words and the ability to think on your feet. Given these, plus an understanding of what you are trying to accomplish, you should not have a great deal of trouble. You should be able to devise original announcements for almost any kind of a program.

CHAPTER FOUR

HUMOR

During the time that you have been plodding through this book, no doubt you have been asking yourself, "How can I be funny? How do I wow an audience with laughter?"

Unfortunately, there are no simple, easy rules to achieve this desired result. To be quite honest about it, both humor and originality are the products of something that cannot be bought in a book. But with a basic talent plus a few suggestions which can be offered, it should not be too difficult to do a reasonably effective job in this department.

The Easy Way

You can tell stories if you want to, but the process of laboriously sifting through ten million jokes to find one suitable for the occasion seems too difficult to be borne. There are books filled with jokes of all kinds. They are listed under subject matter, such as "Matrimony," "Mother-in-Law," and so on. But it seems easier to dwell on home-style situation comedy whenever you can.

Find out what is funny about your audience, your speaker, or his subject. Make your own contribution to posterity by devising a humorous approach to one of these subjects, keeping in mind all the while that brevity is the soul of wit. Deliver your comments with a consistently cheerful countenance and you will get a reasonable number of laughs.

Delivery

Pausing for laughs without seeming to do so is one of the most important things that you have to do when trying to get them. Unless you give your audience time to laugh, its members will "dry up" on you because each person will keep quiet in trying to hear what you have to say next. Pause while the audience laughs. Then start again before the laughter dies entirely away.

Also to keep the audience laughing, you should give some reaction to your own allegedly funny remark, an arrested gestture or a facial expression; although if you are working alone as a speaker or monologist, such a reaction must be very slight. In handling something like the introduction to Fudnuk, the mythical poultry raiser, the remark about the rooster laying the egg should be followed by a slight pause. Then your facial expression should register surprise—surprise that anyone should have brought up the subject.

It is your reaction, tiny though it may be, that really gets the laugh. It confirms your audience in the viewpoint that what they heard was intended to be funny. Therefore they feel much safer in giving way to the release of laughter.

Lest this seem like belaboring the point, watch sometime while an inexperienced person is telling a story in public. Watch when he reaches the point. If it is a good story and the audience fails to laugh, you will observe in almost every instance that the speaker failed to react. The audience received no sign.

The individual in an audience is part of a group. He does not act alone because if there is a laugh, it might be turned on him. Therefore you have to carry the entire group along; you have to make sure that everyone hears and understands the story and knows when the point arrives. Unless you do, the results may be grim.

Professional comedians rarely make this mistake. By offering a funny reaction, they are certain that the audience knows when to laugh; although here, as in everything, a speaker has to be careful. It does not pay to overdo.

Many people, telling a funny story for the first time, expect the story to carry itself. They put nothing into it. They go drowsing along until they reach the point, and then they tell that without any emphasis either. The response is usually a dull and lead-like silence.

Stories have to be told with animation. You have to tell them with an appreciation of their various points as you go along although you should never indicate by either manner or tone that you think the story is funny. Let the audience make that discovery for themselves. Be explicit so that there is no doubt as to what the story is all about.

When you get to the point deliver it with punch and dramatic effect. Hand it out on a shovel. React fast. Then if the audience still fails to laugh, you will at least have the satisfaction of knowing that it was not all your fault.

Timing is important, too. In many treatises on the subject, timing is treated as though it were a highly mysterious endowment, something you either possessed or could not hope to achieve.

True, a sense of timing is inherent with some people and its use can be developed to the point where it seems almost uncanny. But timing is merely the ability to feel the extent of understanding on the part of your audience. If you are certain the audience understands the situation that prevails before you unleash the point of the joke, you can safely tell the point with reasonable assurance that it will be understood.

Good timing is often achieved by an arrangement of words. By arranging the last sentence of the joke—the "snapper"— in such a way that the key word comes near the end, the element of surprise is increased and adds to the quantity of the laugh.

Conversely, if you destroy the laugh-provoking order of the words in the last line of a joke, you are not going to get the laugh either. To illustrate: Take the old joke "Who was that lady I seen you with?" If the last line reads, "That was my wife. She ain't no lady," half the humor of the joke is lost. By keeping the word "wife" at the very end of the sentence as in the original version—"That ain't no lady. That was my wife."—you keep the laugh-getting word where it belongs, at the point nearest where you expect the audience to laugh.

Extensible Stories

Every master of ceremonies should have a collection of extensible stories—that is to say, stories which can be made either short or long as the occasion demands. You will not find these stories listed under any such category in the public library but, from the sample given here, you should be able to recognize one when you see or hear it.

Extensible stories are particularly useful when you have to fill a space on the program because of a delay of some sort. They can be used while equipment is being placed or while the chairman in charge of arrangements, assisted by the hotel porter, tries to find out why the motion picture machine failed to operate as scheduled.

Whatever the situation, launch into your story as artfully as possible. Also, if you are using a long one, do not depend upon a single point. Arrange a few minor laughs along the way while you work toward the big punch line at the end.

Something like the following might be used.

You know, a master of ceremonies, if that is what I am, has to have a good collection of stories. They need not be funny because they are used primarily to fill up the time while eighteen men behind you change the scenery, as they are doing now.

The story I have in mind has a peculiar odor to it because it concerns a skunk.

Here the embroidery begins, and you can make the story as long or as short as you wish.

My story, however, is about a nice skunk—one with a sweet disposition, for a skunk. As a matter of fact, she was a mother skunk, and since she was a mother, she had a heart of gold.

That, though, is not important. The thing to remember is that good old Mother Skunk had two little skunks. One was named Out and the other In.

Now Out and In were two happy little skunks. All day long Out and In ran in and out of their little hole in the ground, until it made Mother Skunk very nervous. She never could tell which skunk was out and which was in.

One time Out would come in and In would go out, until it all got very confusing, or they would reverse the process, with Out out and

In in or, perhaps, it was the other way around. They kept this up, with one or the other of the little skunks going in or out, until poor Mother Skunk could stand it no longer.

Matters, which had been going from bad to worse, finally came to a head one dark and rainy day. The wind blew and the rain come down in torrents. Now it so happened that Out was in and In was out, and this had a very depressing effect on Mother Skunk because In was the most tender of the two little skunks and the one most apt to catch cold.

Finally when Mother Skunk could stand it no longer, she decided that something simply had to be done. She sent Out out to bring In in. Fortunately Out was very lucky and brought In back in a matter of moments. "How did you ever manage to find him so quickly?" Mother Skunk asked in surprise. "Oh, that was easy," Out replied. "In-stinct!"

As can be seen, such a story, and many others like it, can be tailored to fit almost any length of time.

The Search for Stories

It can prove very disheartening if you sit down some dismal day with a pile of joke books or magazines and try to discover jokes that are really funny. Such a method of working will either convince you of the low estate of American humor or you will make the common discovery that only about one joke in ten is really suitable for oral delivery.

Rather than waste your time in this fashion, you will find it easier to take such stories as come your way in the normal course of reading or living. If someone tells you a good story, or you see one printed in a newspaper or a magazine, add it to your collection, provided that it fits your style.

You must be rather careful, however, when selecting stories in this manner. If you hear the same story repeated two or three times, the chances are that it is going the rounds and everyone in your audience will have heard it. Likewise, if it has appeared recently in one of the more commonly-read national magazines, you can also be sure that it will be a mistake to use that story within two or three months following publication. Your audience may remember its source.

Use stories before everyone has had a chance to become familiar with them or wait until everyone has had a chance to forget. Either way, you will find that it is quite easy to maintain a fund of fresh and usable stories.

It is not essential that you maintain a file of jokes that is new and strictly up to date. Older stories have their uses, too. As a matter of fact, there are no really new stories. They are all variations of the same half dozen or so basic themes. Tell a story that is too new, and it is almost certain to fail. The real art in story telling lies in deciding when a story is new enough to be fresh and not so new that it shocks an audience with its originality. You have to use very keen judgment in this regard.

Keeping a Record

A big problem lies in remembering so ephemeral a thing as a joke.

Probably you have heard of gag files, which contain collections of jokes numbering into the hundreds, used by professional jokesmiths and humorists. These jokes are typed on three-by-five cards and filed under headings like "Acrobats," "Aeroplanes," and so on. The real difficulty in such a file lies in the discovery that the best anecdote involving an aeroplane may also come under a heading such as "Heaven." You have to cross-file, listing the same joke under several different headings until, by the time you are through, you may have listed the same joke seventeen or eighteen times and still not be able to find it.

If you are going into the joke business seriously, such labors may be worth your while. But if you are the on-again, off-again type of master of ceremonies, you will find it much more convenient to keep a small pocket-sized, loose-leaf notebook in which you can type a few of the gags that appeal to you. Keep the jokes listed under a few appropriate headings. Always keep the book with you, and by a little juggling you can adapt almost any one of the jokes to fit the situation you have in hand.

Take the following story, for instance.

For years, a restauranteur had watched while the town's leading gourmet had eaten at the restaurant across the street. Finally one day the restaurant owner, watching from the window, saw the gourmet heading for the restaurant owner's establishment. He enjoined the waiter to give the gourmet the best that the house afforded.

Finally, after the gourmet had eaten and paid his check, the restaurant owner asked how he had enjoyed the meal. "Fine!" the gourmet said. "But not enough bread."

When he had left, the restaurant owner asked the waiter to make sure that the next time the gourmet came into the restaurant that he got enough bread. The next time he came in for dinner, the waiter piled on half a dozen slices of bread.

Again as he paid his bill and started to leave, the restaurant owner asked the gourmet how he had enjoyed his meal. "Fine," he replied. "Only not enough bread."

The next time the restaurant owner was determined to see that their distinguished visitor got enough bread. But it was several days, even weeks, before the gourmet came in again.

Finally one evening just about closing time, the restaurant owner was looking out of the window again when, lo and behold, he saw the gourmet coming down the street, headed in the direction of the restaurant. The establishment was out of bread!

Hurriedly he sent the waiter rushing out into the street to the town's only bakery to see if he could get some bread. But the only thing he could find at that late hour was a loaf of French bread about six feet long. The waiter rushed back to the restaurant, where the gourmet was already eating. Breaking the long loaf of bread in two, he placed the two pieces on the table. The gourmet continued his meal and, when he had finished, the restaurant owner went up to the cashier with him while he was paying the bill. "How did you like the dinner?" he asked.

"Fine," the gourmet replied.

"How about the bread?" the restaurant owner asked.

"It was fine, too," the gourmet replied. "But why only two pieces?"

Such a story can be used to illustrate a number of points. Before an assembly of bakers, it could be used to illustrate the idea of eating more bread. Before general groups, it could be used to illustrate how difficult it is to please people. Its possibilities are endless. By adding comments at the end or at the beginning, you adapt the story to fit your own particular needs.

Pre-testing

Never put a joke in your book for public use without testing it beforehand. Tell it to your friends, either singly or in small groups. You may lose all your friends, but you will also wind up with an excellent collection of jokes.

If your friends laugh, if you find that you have the faculty for telling that particular joke, put it away in your collection for proper aging. Then, when a reasonable length of time has elapsed, take it out for use when everyone, including your friends, has forgotten all about it.

As you go along adding new jokes, canvass the old ones, deleting those which have served their purpose, or you can, if you wish, store them away for four or five years, when they may turn out to be just as good as new.

Jokes to Avoid

In the search for humor, there is one form you can happily neglect. Dialect stories, because they so often cast aspersions on another's race or creed, are falling into the discard. You will still run across them, but the public is so constantly being lectured about racial intolerance that many people are becoming a little self-conscious about this type of humor. It still survives, but you will do well not to use it or, if you do, select only those specimens which do not place another's race or nationality in a derogatory light.

At the same time, skip those stories which depend upon profanity to make a point. The moment you start using profanity you are certain to start losing your audience. Clean up those stories in which it appears.

In a similar category are the so-called blue gags—suggestive stories which depend upon sex as their principal ingredient. Stories of this type are rarely successful even when employed by a master of ceremonies at a stag smoker, and you are better off not to use them.

From a purely technical standpoint, there is another type of joke which you should avoid. This is the he-and-she joke.

For example: **He**—So you're going home to Mother? **She (sarcastically)**—No, dear, Mother is coming home with me.

Such stories can be made to work if you tell them with another person, as when you act the part of a straight man with a comedian, but they are rarely successful when you tell them alone. They must be revised. Besides, they are a little out of style.

When working before the average banquet or dinner audience, what you need is jokes that have a little color and background to them. You need stories that illustrate the points you are trying to make. You need stories that have action—stories that can be told with animation and gestures.

Here is an example:

A friend of mine was not feeling well. He decided to go to the doctor. "Doctor," he said, "I don't know what's the matter with me, but I feel that the front of my suit is covered with feathers." (*Business of brushing feathers off the front of the suit.*)

"I'm sorry," the doctor said, "But I don't handle this kind of illness. It's all mental. I'll take you down the hall to where there's a psychiatrist. He's a good friend of mine, and I'm sure he'll be able to help you."

So the doctor took my friend down the hall. He was ushered into the presence of the great man, and he said, "Doctor, I'm sorry to bother you with a thing like this. I realize that it's only mental, but I seem to feel that the front of my suit is covered with feathers." (*Business of again brushing the imaginary feathers from the front of the suit.*)

"Well, be careful!" the psychiatrist shouted. "Don't get them on me!" (*Acting very alarmed and again brushing the feathers from the front of the suit*).

This joke is more than vocal. It has action which can be fitted to the word, and such jokes, with beginners, are easier to put across than jokes which depend upon vocal timing alone.

No joke, even the best one, should be dragged in without a reason. You have doubtless seen or heard of the embryo speaker who has read somewhere that one is supposed to tell a few stories at the beginning of a speech, in order to warm the audience up. He then proceeds to tell a few, with results that are lamentable. He had no sense of the fitness of things. Instead of using the stories for the enjoyment of the audience, he was trying to make things easier for himself. Such a philosophy seldom works when you are dealing with other people.

For instance, in the story about the psychiatrist, it could be used to illustrate the point that even an expert can have his shortcomings. But "our speaker this evening, ladies and gentlemen, has a world-wide reputation for proficiency in his field. There are no feathers on him!"

By handling stories in such a fashion, you make them pay double value. They get a laugh, and they also serve as a handle by means of which you can get a good grip on whatever it is you are trying to accomplish.

Rebuilding Stories

You are much better off if you try to provide your own comic comments on any situation you meet. To be quite honest about it, however, it is not everyone who can dream up snappy rejoinders. If you have difficulty in this respect, try to revise such jokes as you can find. You may be able to make them meet the situation more closely and, with a little experience, you can quickly learn how the process works.

Take the pale specimen mentioned earlier — the he-and-she joke. With a little effort, even it can be revised until it might be possible to get a laugh. For example: "She was a modern, independent woman. She'd never think of going home to mother, whatever the pretext. Instead, she'd bring her mother home with her. In that way, the old man would lose double—once, by having her in the house, second, by having to play canasta with her."

A fertile source of jokes lies in those volumes containing quotations from various sources. Some of these are humorous in themselves but oftentimes with a little fixing they can be turned into humorous comments. For instance, the following: "Lincoln is credited with saying, 'It has ever been my experience that folks who have no vices have very few virtues.' All of which worries me about our speaker this evening. He has so many virtues that I wonder what he is like when he is alone. I am sure that any vices he has must be secret, because I have been unable to detect them myself."

Through working in this fashion, you may take some very old material and reshape it to suit your purposes admirably.

Recoveries

No matter how good you are at telling stories, there are bound to be times when some of them fall flat as a disappointed waffle. They simply do not "go over," and you will be greeted by silence as cold and vast as that at the Arctic Circle. When that happens, do not stand and stare vacantly at your audience as though you had suddenly remembered something naughty you had done as a child.

The wise master of ceremonies will be prepared. He will have a couple of snappy recovery lines available, so he can use them when the need arises.

You have heard performers on the radio say, "Thank you, relatives!" when only a few people cackled at the back of the studio. Try to come up with original items of your own. Here are a pair of useful though uninspired specimens: "It sounded funny when I tried it out on my mother-in-law" and "My wife liked it when I told it at home." By leaping into the breach with a sure-fire laugh getter, you may be able to salvage a situation that might otherwise prove to be very embarrassing.

Of course, you can use such a recovery method only once or twice in an evening. After that, you had better stop telling stories.

Hecklers

Sooner or later you will come face to face with a heckler—some obnoxious little person in the back of the hall who thinks he is funnier than you are. Drunk or sober, he is a nuisance.

Hecklers you can afford to ignore the first time around, unless you have either an appropriate or a laugh-provoking answer. The second time, however, that one of these pests tries to get under your skin, you had better try to do something about it or you may lose the respect of your audience. Do it gently but firmly, so the person involved will be inclined to keep quiet for the rest of the evening.

Usually the mere recognition that you have heard the heckler will be enough, because the audience invariably will be on your side. Say something like, "That's very funny, son, but that ain't the way I heard it" or "If anyone else wishes to recite, please hold up your hand."

Devise stoppers of your own and have them ready at the tip of your tongue, but never get angry. That is what the heckler is trying to accomplish—to make you angry. If he succeeds, he has won the argument, regardless of anything you can say.

One Final Word

The following little story illustrates as well as anything one of the things you must remember about humor.

A new inmate was being indoctrinated at state's prison and the warden was being very careful to explain that he was running a model prison—one where every effort was made to keep the prisoners happy. As a climax to the conversation, the warden gave the new man a book of jokes, which he was to take to his cell with him. The new man read the book and discovered that most of the jokes were exceedingly funny.

Later that night, he was astonished to hear the various prisoners yelling at one another along the cell block. One man would call out, "Forty-eight!" another, "Fifty-two!" and after each of these sallies, the other prisoners would laugh uproariously.

The situation had the new man confused, so the next morning he asked permission to go down and talk to the warden. "Why is it, Warden," he asked, "that when the fellows call out those different numbers, everybody laughs?"

"That's easy," the warden replied. "All of those jokes I gave you in that book are numbered. When a man yells a number, the others can visualize the joke, too, and they laugh."

That night the new man thought he would join in the fun. "Sixty-one!" he yelled. Nothing happened. "Forty-nine!" Dead silence again.

Next morning the new man cornered one of the older inmates on the rock pile. "Say, buddy," he asked, "how is that when those other fellows yell the numbers they laugh? When I do it, they keep as silent as the tomb. What's the matter?"

"Oh, you know how it is," the old hand replied. "Some guys can tell 'em and some can't!"

CHAPTER FIVE

PHYSICAL DEPORTMENT

Probably until this moment you thought it was only necessary to wander in front of your audience in any reasonably upright position and let fly with your bright remarks. It is not that easy, if you want to do a good job. There is a discipline in physical movement as in everything else.

How to Dress

Before describing how to put one foot ahead of another, it might be well to digress for a moment and discuss the kind of clothing which ought to be worn under varying circumstances.

Periodically all professional masters of ceremonies show up wearing the same types of costumes. At one moment, they will all wear midnight blue dress suits of an exaggerated cut and the next, they will wear sack suits and battered felt hats and all will be puffing on long black cigars. It all depends on who most recently made a hit as a master of ceremonies and how he dressed. All the others will imitate him.

For best results, however, you will avoid these stereotypes and dress according to the particular kind of work you have to do. Make sure that the clothes you wear are good of their kind, well cut, and of reasonably good material. They need not be expensive, but it pays to choose accessories with care.

At a businessmen's luncheon, wear a business suit. When a tuxedo or more formal dress is appropriate, wear either one or the other, but make sure that whatever you wear is in the best of condition. Not only do you look better in clothes that are correctly chosen and well cared for, but they help to impart a feeling of spruceness and a confidence in your work that might not otherwise be present.

As a general rule, do not wear clothes that are too conservative in cut or pattern. If you are the principal speaker, a dull gray may be more suitable, but when you are the master of ceremonies, a little more life in the costume is not amiss. Women, too, should follow the same sort of rules when selecting a wardrobe.

Their clothes should not be elaborate. In fact, it is better if they are kept rather simple and smart in appearance, although here again accessories can be extremely important. Choose those accessories which lend an air of distinction to the dress. They should neither be too large nor too bright nor should they contain any features that unduly attract the attention of the audience. Corsages, if worn, should be kept rather small.

Solid colors are best. Prints are all right if the design is small, formal, and indistinct. Do not wear a dress with bold patterns or scenes or figures printed on it or the audience may spend most of the time trying to figure out what the motion pictures are all about.

For women appearing at luncheon meetings, a simple suit or plain dress is the best. For grander affairs, a dinner dress or formal gown can be worn, but these should be neither too extreme nor too daring. If the latter, the audience may be more interested in watching the dress than in listening to what its wearer has to say. Dresses worn on the stage or on an elevated platform should be selected with care, to make sure that the skirt is of the proper length to appear graceful.

If a play, a revue, or a similar entertainment is presented, it may prove desirable to have the master of ceremonies— either a man or woman—appear in a costume more in keeping with the proceedings. But here again it seldom pays to go to the extreme. The master of ceremonies should be identified with the audience and not with the production. For that reason, the master of ceremonies most often appears in a tuxedo, regardless of the costumes worn by the rest of the cast.

At Luncheon or Dinner

It is assumed that you are now sitting on the edge of your

chair, the top of your mouth as dry and tasteless as a piece of old flannel. You are leaning forward, prepared to rise to your feet, and you are wondering whether you will be able to accomplish the trick without falling flat on your face. Taking one last glimpse at your audience out of the corner of one eye, you swallow hard and propel yourself upward. Immediately when you get to your feet, you are faced with a problem. Should you push your chair back and leave it there, or should you stand in back of it, using the chair as a kind of support? The temptation is great to stand with your hands anchored to the back of the chair, but do not yield to it.

By leaving the chair two or three feet in back of the table, you reduce the number of movements necessary in rising and sitting because you do not have to move the chair. You will also discover that, by sitting a few feet in back of the table, you are better able to keep track of what is going on to either side of you without turning your head. Finally when you rise, you have more room in which to gesture—something you cannot do with your hands tied to the back of the chair.

With the chair two or three feet in back of the table, you, figuratively speaking, retire from the scene each time you sit down. Also you will be able to accomplish more inconspicuously those little odd jobs which are certain to fall to the lot of any master of ceremonies.

Keep your notes lying on the table. Glance at them from time to time, or, if you have to, lean forward and take them quietly while another speaker is talking.

Try not to hold your notes in your hand while making an introduction. If someone hands you unfamiliar material, like the name of a person wanted on the telephone, it is all right to read the note, but it is better not to do so, if you possibly can.

To command attention, use a gavel, although a public address system, if available, may be all that you need. The sound of your voice, roaring over the horns, may be all that is required to quiet the audience at the start of the program. You may not have to use a gavel but, remember, it is extremely difficult to get attention by rapping on the side of a glass with a spoon. Besides, it looks and sounds a trifle silly.

If you do not have a gavel of your own, make sure that the organization before which you are to appear provides you with one. Many times, such implements are a part of the dinner equipment at hotels and restaurants where banquets are held. Ask for one if it seems to be missing. The mere presence of a gavel is a deterrent to unseemly interruptions, and it should be used when necessary.

Do not pound too loudly with the gavel, especially at the beginning. Tap lightly but authoritatively two or three times. Then wait with a slight smile on your face while the audience chooses to stop the conversation. If you do it with sufficient confidence, you will be amazed at how quickly the average audience quiets down and gives you its wholehearted attention.

Recently, there has been a tendency to deprecate the more formal aspects of being a master of ceremonies. But courtesy, if it be sincere, still pays off. Also audiences prefer that those appearing before them do so with a certain amount of finesse.

When introducing the speaker, do not do so and then sit down as though you had discharged your responsibility. Wait until the speaker has risen to his feet and acknowledge any bow or smile that he or she may direct to you. Listen, too, in case any remark is addressed to you. Do not relax until the speaker has launched into his discourse. Even then it pays to keep listening, with at least one ear, in the event that something turns up that you might be able to use.

At the end, be prompt in getting to your feet, look at the speaker with a grateful smile, and be vigorous in the way you lead the applause.

Before the Microphone

If a microphone is needed, there are several rules concerning its use which, if followed, will help you to avoid appearing like a novice. Most modern microphones are sensitive enough so that it is not necessary to bellow directly into them. In fact, the voice quality may improve if the mouth is kept a few inches away from the instrument.

That being true, use good judgment when facing a microphone. If you do not "crowd" it, there will be less tendency to "blast." Stand back and let the amplifier do a little of the work. It is equally important that you do not stand with the microphone directly in front of your face. It makes you look like an ant-eater, with the ears sticking out. Stand to one side, or better yet, have the microphone lowered to the level of your shoulders and speak over it—an arrangement which permits some facial expression to remain visible to the audience. The microphone, too, should be as small as possible. Great cumbersome things are no longer needed and should be consigned to the junk heap.

At many dinners, there will be an extra problem, occasioned by the presence of only one microphone for a number of speakers. It means normally that all of them will have to use the same piece of equipment.

Clear a large space behind the head table and around the microphone by moving the chairs back. All of the speakers then have easy access to the machine without congestion or awkwardness, and you can keep a chair for yourself conveniently placed where you can reach the instrument and still stay out of the line of traffic. Incidentally, when one speaker uses a microphone, all should use it. Otherwise, the audience must make too much of an adjustment between the various speakers to enjoy the program.

At those happy affairs where more than one microphone is provided, two can do a superior job. One can be left with the toastmaster or master of ceremonies, while the second— a small table microphone—can be moved along to the next speaker. However, it is best to have the speakers arranged in order, or the microphone will have to be passed back and forth like a relay baton, causing a good deal of confusion. In any event, it is not essential to have more than one microphone, if arrangements are properly made beforehand.

Check your own voice level to make certain that you can be heard. If possible, have the other people on the program check their voice levels, too. Make a note of any adjustments that have to be made in the height of the microphone and change its position during your own introduction rather than delay the start of the next number.

If a technician is present, listen to what he has to tell you about the functioning of the sound system, and you will be happier. These men are paid to do a good job, and you will be much better off if you follow their suggestions.

If you are lucky, you may discover that a lapel microphone has been provided, a small button microphone which fastens to the lapel of your coat. When this happens, you can ignore the microphone almost completely, except for the cord which trails behind you wherever you go. When you start for the wings after making an announcement on the stage, be careful not to stumble over the cord. Better make sure, too, that it does not get in the way of other performers or get hooked around the legs of chairs or other protuberances.

On occasions where it becomes necessary to move a stand microphone, especially on the stage, do so as inconspicuously as possible. Make the move during your own introduction, rather than inconvenience the next act or speaker who must use the microphone in its new position.

Check also to make sure if it is necessary for you to change the height of the microphone. Unless you do, you may have to run out on the stage and change the height of the microphone for a performer who is unable to do it for himself.

In a radio or television studio, the situation is somewhat different. The emphasis is on what goes out over the air and not what happens in the studio. Should a studio audience be present, however, it does no harm to follow some of the suggestions made above. But only rarely will you be permitted to move equipment in a radio or television studio. That privilege is reserved for the technicians in charge and not for the casual visitor.

In the Cabaret

You are now asking yourself, "Why should I know anything about appearing in a cabaret?"

True, you may never be a master of ceremonies in a night club or cabaret. But there are certain distinct advantages in knowing a little about the style and how to handle it when the need arises. Roughly, any place where the actors or entertainers work with the audience seated on all four sides or on three is a cabaret. Nowadays, such an arrangement is oftentimes called an arena theater, but that term refers most often to a drama or musical play. Cabarets present a more informal type of entertainment—vaudeville or revues. Frequently the audience are seated at tables but, for the purposes of this discussion, tables are not essential.

You will meet the problem most often in lodge halls, where the audience is seated around the perimeter of the room with you in the center. The idea is to work in such a manner that you avoid turning your back to any large segment of the audience at any one time. Since this arrangement proves impossible without turning yourself into a whirling dervish, you effect a kind of compromise. You reach a working agreement with your audience by keeping your back most of the time to the door by which you entered the playing space.

You thus escape the impoliteness of striding out upon the floor and then deliberately turning your back on any part of the audience. Later, as occasion permits, you turn one way or the other to include different sections of the audience in your remarks. In this manner, you keep from slighting anyone, and you run less risk of losing your mind through attempting to talk to everyone at the same time.

By now though you are doubtless asking, "Why bother? If there is so much difficulty about talking to everyone at once, why not carry on the program in the conventional manner and forget all about the cabaret style?"

There may be a certain justice in this position, but there are also advantages to be discovered in the other way of doing things. First, you are closer to the audience. A more intimate approach is possible, and you will find it a great deal easier to get a response. Second, you will be amazed at how many times the cabaret style can turn an otherwise stuffy entertainment into something not completely a waste of time. If the entertainers have never done anything of the sort before, they develop an entirely new approach to their material, and an added feeling of freshness results.

Frequently you will find yourself performing in halls which are not well adapted to the type of entertainment in hand. Church basements, for instance, are often so cluttered with pillars that it is quite impossible to present an ordinary banquet program without someone's vision being blocked. Rather than ask the audience to move, whenever the structure of the hall makes it possible, move the entertainment instead and adopt the cabaret style. The audience will bless you because many of them may not have been able either to see or hear under the previous arrangement.

If you preside at a dance, on one of those soul-trying occasions when you are expected to present entertainment at the intermission, the most feasible way of doing so is right on the dance floor, with the audience resting its weary feet on the sidelines. The entertainment can be handled very much as in a cabaret, though a word of warning is here in order.

Entertainment of any kind is rarely successful when presented during the intermission at a dance. People want to powder their noses, or do other things. The entertainment committee which insists on providing something during this period is only wasting its money. If they insist on this course, however, suggest that the entertainment be staged before the dance begins.

But there is still another virtue in the cabaret style. If you are called in beforehand by the harried entertainment committee, you can frequently change the haunted look in its members' eyes to one of sheer joy by suggesting that they consider the virtues of the cabaret style. Since they will not have thought of that idea themselves, or at least will not have called it by that name, they will look upon you as a positive genius and will doubtless stand for a raise in fee, if you are working for money.

The Stage

You will have to have more snap and polish to be successful as a master of ceremonies on the stage than in any other phase of the business. You will have to work more rapidly and with more force and precision.

All of which should bring you to a consideration of the first fact you should remember about your physical deportment on the stage. You cannot be hesitant. You have to be wherever you are going the moment the psychological moment arrives, or you will throw a big wet blanket over everything you are trying to do. This rule applies to every phase of the business, but the strict observance of it is more necessary on the stage than in any other place.

Practice walking on the balls of your feet. Move rapidly and with quick, energetic strides. Never permit a moment of indecision to mar your movement, if you can help it. Make up your mind exactly where you are going and get there with promptness and despatch.

These are general rules. There are others which are more specific. The rules can be varied somewhat to suit yourself, but the same general principles outlined here will apply to most of your work, even though they are most important when working on the stage.

Assume that you are introducing a new act. You are standing, not at stage center but, perhaps, one third of the distance from stage right. Your position gives more of the stage to the on-coming act, even before it appears, because the new act will be making an entrance from stage left. By giving stage, by standing a little off center, you prepare the audience to welcome whatever is coming to fill the space on the stage, because audiences, like nature, abhor a vacuum. In other words, you always give stage, at least slightly, in the opposite direction from the side of the stage where the act is making its appearance.

After making the introduction, you leave the stage as rapidly as possible, but not before directing the attention of the audience toward the oncoming act, either by a bow, a smile, or a wave of the hand.

Unless the act is well known and established, it is not too good an idea to force a welcoming burst of applause before the act begins. It is better to let the act get started and show its own merits without any special help from you, although here the exception may only prove the rule. Insisting upon a welcome at all times only forces the issue and slows down the progress of the entertainment.

At the conclusion, your appearance to lead the applause can have a great deal to do with the amount received. Appear too soon, and your sudden propulsion upon the scene may so distract the audience that the applause never gets started. Arrive too late, and the applause may die without hope of revival.

You will not have been in front of an audience very long before you discover that applause is like a wave. It rises rapidly, reaching its crest in a very short time. Then more slowly it dies away. At the psychological moment, when the applause has reached its peak and the instant before it starts to slide down into the trough, you appear.

What you do, therefore, is related to the reaction of the audience and not to the work of the act. On the stage, however, you will find that your most appropriate moment for projecting yourself upon the scene is the instant before the actors start to leave after taking their second bow.

Such a procedure, of course, presupposes that the actors know how to take a bow. With amateurs, it may be best to appear after they have left the stage at the conclusion of their first bow. If the actors themselves are unfamiliar with the technique of gaining applause, it may be necessary for you to appear earlier to save the act from its own weaknesses.

Do not, however, try to force encores or to revive applause that has already fallen too far. Such a course tires the audience and makes it reluctant to applaud when an act really deserves the added attention. Get all the applause you can, but the instant before the audience shows it has had enough, stop and proceed with the next introduction.

When moving around, be sure and re-enter the stage from the same side on which you left. To leave at right and then re-enter from the left will only confuse the audience and may result in a diminished quantity of applause, while a few thoughtful souls out front try to figure out how you got from one side of the stage to the other.

If you do change entrances—and you should frequently, to add variety to your appearances—make the change after introducing the act, and when you leave the stage. Then come back from the same side of the stage after the act is over. In this way, you keep changing your position without making it too obvious. In other words, you must move to a new position each time you make an introduction or take stage center, and the actors must enter from the opposite side of the stage, in order to keep things in balance. It all sounds very complicated, but once tried out on the stage, you will find that it works quite easily.

On the stage or anywhere else, for that matter, the worst failing of the beginning or amateur master of ceremonies is to permit the members of an act to take too many bows or encores. As a result, the entire show suffers and those performers who have the misfortune to come near the end of the program must face an audience which is already worn out from applauding. There should be discretion in this respect.

If an act gets a moderate amount of applause, let the actors take an extra bow. If the audience insists, permit an encore, but only one, though it is permissible to take another bow after an encore if the audience is especially insistent. Anything more than that is apt to spell the ruination of whatever follows and spoil the show.

Under most conditions, the master of ceremonies should be the sole judge of whether an act deserves an encore or not.

If, however, there is a stage manager or director, a brief nod from him or a shake of the head will aid the master of ceremonies in reaching a decision.

To keep things moving, it may be wise even to kill applause but, with a genuine "show stopper," there will be very little you can do. Killing applause is done through movement. You can, if you wish, attempt to announce the next number by bellowing over a drumfire of applause from those hardy spirits who want more of the same. But this course smacks too much of shouting down the opposition to be either polite or effective. Besides, since the eye is quicker than the ear, you can more readily kill applause with action than you can with words.

Move either to the right or left, as though preparing to introduce the next act, but do it more forcefully than usual. Unless your audience is completely unpredictable, they will stop applauding to see what it is you have in mind.

If you try to talk, do not shout. Let the applause drown you out, but make sure that the audience sees that your lips are moving. Unless the situation is already out of control, invariably they will stop applauding to see what it is you have to say. Then when silence reigns, you go ahead and repeat that part of your announcement which was drowned out by the applause. No one will know that you have engaged in this bit of trickery.

Naturally you do not go about killing applause merely to find out how it is done. The only legitimate time that you can kill applause is when the actors are too exhausted to continue, as with tap dancers, or when the act fails to have material which can be used as an encore. The rest of the time you are principally concerned with getting as much applause as you possibly can.

As a general rule you should shorten applause at the beginning of a show in order that the audience has something left for the end. Do not permit an audience to exhaust itself with countless encores early in a program, when there may be other numbers later that are equally worthy of attention.

These precautions are especially important when there are children on the program. If they appear early—and they frequently do—the audience may applaud itself silly and have nothing left for the acts which follow.

The Law of Quietness

Unless the beginning master of ceremonies has been thoroughly schooled in the discipline of the stage, he has one more thing to remember: Bodily movements that are unrelated to the purpose in hand tend to be distracting and cut down on the quantity of applause.

Do not jitter about the stage. Stand still when you are not walking and when you are walking go some place and stop. Do not make unnecessary movements with your hands or feet. In watching these flitting members, the audience may become so fascinated that they forget to applaud.

Anything you do must have a purpose. Here is a safe rule: Unless the movement you have in mind is designed to accomplish something specific, do not make it. Stand still and concentrate on moving your audience to laughter, to tears, or to a greater degree of appreciation. By adding these refinements to your art, you increase its effectiveness and add to your own enjoyment in your work.

CHAPTER SIX

ATHLETIC EVENTS

Public address announcing at sporting events is not always considered work for a master of ceremonies. If, however, you are reasonably adept at any phase of making public introductions, you can expect, sooner or later, to be asked to perform before a sporting crowd. The home-town basketball game, the track meet, the Saturday football game are all grist for the mill. Therefore it is well to know something about the job and some of the pitfalls that lie ahead of you.

Hazards of the Course

The public address announcer at any athletic event is doubly vulnerable. He must tell enough about what is going on for the benefit of those who know nothing about sports and, at the same time, he must be careful not to insult the intelligence of the dyed-in-the-wool sports fans, lest they descend on him in a horde and destroy him.

If you think this task is simple, you are due for a rude awakening. No one is quite so vindictive as the sports fan who feels that justice has not been done to one of his heroes. So if you must ignore anyone, ignore the uninitiated. Illogical as this sounds, it may be your best road to survival.

To avoid getting yourself into trouble with the rabid sports fan—that is the question. The best way is to stay at home. The next best way is to know more about sports than the average fan. But since this is manifestly impossible, you adopt another method entirely.

You provide yourself with nose-bleed insurance in the form of two extra precautions. First, when in front of the microphone at a sporting event, you never say more than is absolutely necessary. You will be surprised to see how much this precaution reduces the possibility of error. Second, if you are not too familiar with the sport under consideration, have someone sit beside you who is fairly expert—someone who can advise you on the proper thing to say when the need arises. By pursuing these two courses, you will find that you can get along quite successfully and with reasonable assurance of living to a healthy old age.

General Procedure

If you are announcing team sports, pay a visit to the individual dressing rooms before each contest and get the probable starting line-ups from the hands of the coaches. Make the visit at the earliest possible moment. Coaches disturbed as late as half an hour before game time have a habit of growling at you like wounded bears.

Check such information as you will need about the individual players—weights, etc. Above all, check to see if anyone has achieved the horrendous idea of changing the numbers or uniforms of the players.

It is amazing how often the following happens: You sit in front of the microphone firmly convinced that everything is under control when, lo and behold, everyone runs out on the field wearing a different number from the one stated on the official program. The teams do not even seem to be wearing the same uniforms you saw them donning in the dressing room. You are appalled. At the last moment, one coach or the other has decided that his uniforms are too similar to those of the opposing team and, as a result, someone might tackle the wrong man or pass the ball to the wrong player. To your horror, you now discover that every player now has a different number or, to make confusion complete, opposing players on different teams are wearing the same number. Teams supposed to be wearing red are now wearing yellow and vice versa. If you are not informed of the change beforehand, you will have to straighten out the mess in the last few minutes before game time—which means that you will start your work halfway on the road to a nervous breakdown.

At most sporting events you will find a printed program

or mimeographed sheet of some kind serving the same purpose. All you need do is pick it up and check the names of the players designated by the coach as his starting line-up.

You will be surprised at the number of times you will have to buy this program for yourself. No one thinks of providing the poor public address announcer with reliable information, not even when he is working for nothing. He has to dig it out for himself.

When doing the digging, remember that most of those involved have worries of their own and are not particularly interested in any of your problems. You will practically have to beat them over the head to get any information at all. But beat them you will if you intend to do a good job.

If the coach is too busy, you may be able to get the information you require from the assistant coach or from the team manager who, in many instances, seems to know more about what is going on than the coach himself.

Usually, too, it is a good idea to get acquainted with the officials in charge—if you do not already know them—and with the heads of the schools or athletic directors, if it is an interscholastic or intercollegiate contest. Ask them if there are any special announcements they would like to have made. Very often if you are provided with such material beforehand, you can space it more judiciously throughout the course of the contest rather than launch it altogether at some particular moment when they might find it convenient to give it to you.

It may sound silly going through these details, but you will discover that your job is eased in direct proportion to the amount of inquiring and leg work you do before the beginning of a contest. Not only will you do a better job, but you may avoid some of those errors which were mentioned earlier.

Individual Sports

Football.—Because of the number of men involved, football is one of the most difficult of all sports to handle. The principal problem lies in having some sort of system for keeping track of the players. The easiest method is to have a board, generally of plywood, in which a number of small nails or brads have been driven. The brads are lined up like opposing players on the two teams.

Names and numbers of the individual players are then printed boldly on small pieces of cardboard with holes punched in them. Then when the line-ups are decided, the pieces of cardboard are hung on the nails in the correct position. As substitutions are made, the cardboard tab with the proper name is placed over the name of the original player. The process is carried on throughout the remainder of the game, with names and numbers being substituted as substitutions are made in the various positions out on the field.

Before the game gets under way, however, it is customary to give the names, weights, and positions played by the men in the starting line-ups. Give the line-up of the visiting team first because, as usually happens, there will be more supporters for the home team. Also this procedure gives the people who arrive late an opportunity to discover who is playing on the home squad.

Give the names of the officials in charge of the game and, if it will add anything to the enjoyment or understanding of the spectators, give a capsulized version of the records of the two teams in league play. If they are close contenders, it may add interest to the coming contest.

During the course of play, you will be expected to keep track of substitutions and announce them as they occur. You will be expected to announce the yardages involved in the various penalties and the reasons for those penalties. As a result, you must familiarize yourself with the hand and arm signals employed by the officials on the field. In addition to keeping track of the time-outs and announcing the name of the team requesting one, you will also have to keep track of the number of yards gained or lost on each play, the position of the ball, and the number of downs and the yards to go, as well as the names of the players immediately involved in each play. You announce the score whenever a change occurs and, in between times, request the grounds keeper to kick a stray dog from the field and ask a policeman to keep a number of freshmen from slaughtering one another in the cheap seats.

From the foregoing you can readily see that at a football game the public address announcer does not have a great deal of time in which to engage in idle dreaming. He is very busy.

As a matter of fact, it is well nigh impossible to do the job without help, customarily in the form of spotters, one from each team. The one from the visiting team should restrict himself to identifying players for you, since you are less apt to be familiar with the burly boys from out of town than you are with the local players. The local spotter can, if he wishes, help you in the other departments. He can, for instance, double check on the number of yards made on a play or on the number of the down, in the event that you temporarily lose yourself and cannot find the ball.

Where do you get spotters? They are recommended to you by the coaches of the teams. In these days of radio and television broadcasting, most coaches have the names of suitable people immediately at hand, and you will soon learn that high school or college students can do an amazingly competent job as spotters. Many of the injured players or second assistant team managers who climb into the booth with you can make the difference between a really fine job and one that is only competent.

The home town and visiting team spotters should remain on the same side as the team they are following. That being true, when the teams shift position at the end of the quarters, the spotters in the booth should shift sides, too. It cuts down confusion and, if your board has been correctly made, all you need do is turn it upside down, and the cardboard tabs will change position, along with the players on the field.

It is not necessary to talk all the time when doing public address work. Far from it! You are not making a radio broadcast or attempting to re-create the whole scene. The spectators present can tell what is going on as well as you can. Restrict yourself to factual information and make this clean cut, clear, and concise.

In these days of big football stadiums, you may find yourself in a steam-heated announcer's booth in direct communication, by wire or short-wave radio, with an assistant who travels along the sidelines and reports to you on downs and yardages directly from the head linesman's position. There are times, however, when you may be expected to function while clinging to a light pole with a twenty-degrees-below-zero snowstorm whistling about your ears.

You are more likely to measure up to the standards you set for yourself by checking the situation thoroughly beforehand, and this means, among other things, that you must be able to see the yard markers clearly. You would be surprised at the number of football fields there are where the public address announcer is expected to announce the yards and downs without being able to see any markers. If you find that that is the case on the field where you work, see if it is possible to move the public address microphone to a spot where you can see. You certainly should be able to see the markers on the opposite side of the field. The congestion on your side will usually make it impossible for you even to guess where the markers are. People running up and down the sidelines are certain to obscure the markers, but with the open football field between you and those on the opposite side, you are able, ordinarily, to see them quite well.

There is one other thing, too, which must be considered when announcing at football games, and that is the half-time activities. You may feel like running out for a quick cup of coffee or munching a hot dog, but you will probably have to stay in your booth or cling to your pole while weirdly assorted people in fancy costumes go through gyrations down on the field.

At all well-organized games, you will be provided with a

script outlining the various formations and the tunes to be played. The script will be provided by the leader of the band, who should be asked to explain in great detail the meaning of the hieroglyphics on the sheet he hands you. It may also prove helpful to have some member of the booster club, faculty adviser, or misplaced tuba player in the booth with you at half-time, so you can announce according to cue and not make any mistakes.

Actually the half-time activities should not prove too difficult to handle, but a little help can be invaluable. It is one thing to read about these activities on a sheet of paper, but quite another to see them enacted on the field. Frequently there will be last-minute changes or things will not turn out as you expected. It pays, therefore, to go over the routine with the band director or with the footloose student who has been assigned to help you in the booth.

You may be asked to introduce dignitaries during the half-time period. The mayor will dedicate a new scoreboard, or someone will make an appeal on behalf of the Community Chest. Be brief! Give all the facts required, but do not waste any words on a flowery introduction. No crowd at a sporting event is going to sit still while you indulge in a long-winded introduction. Say what you have to say, but cut it short!

Dress warmly. At football games in the fall of the year, you can get very cold sitting behind a microphone, where you are not able to move. Keep your throat warm, also, with a wool muffler or scarf around your neck, or your voice may give out before the game is over. Keep your feet warm, too! Wear wool socks and overshoes if there is the slightest doubt of your feet keeping warm. Nothing is more difficult than sitting before a microphone trying to announce when you are cold and uncomfortable.

Baseball.—As with most sports, the amount of information you give over the public address system at a baseball game is governed somewhat by the amount of information displayed on the official scoreboard. If the latter gadget flashes everything but the ancestry of the individual players, you will not be overburdened by the quantity of statistics you have to peddle over the microphone.

Sometimes you will give the line-ups and the names of the officials before the game starts. At other times, you will give only the batteries and the officials. Then, as each man comes to bat, you give his name, position, and sometimes his place in the batting order. For example: "Pogreba, short stop, top of the batting order."

At the conclusion of each half inning, give a summary for the team involved: hits, runs, and errors. If there is no official scoreboard, you may be asked to give a recapitulation of the total score as well. Other than keeping an eye open for such developments as a pinch-hitter or an ear cocked for information sent your way by the official scorer, these constitute your principal duties at a baseball game.

If there are special prizes for the baseball players, you will be asked to handle this assignment, too. You will have to award prizes like a sack of flour donated for the first two-bagger of the game—prizes donated by local merchants in the hope of getting a little advertising. It is a common custom at baseball games, though you will rarely meet with it in other forms of sport, especially those which are considered to be amateur.

Remember, too, that humor is seldom appreciated at baseball games. Save that joke until later. Strictly speaking, you are wiser not to indulge in humor when handling the microphone at any kind of competitive sports event. Passions run high. You may say the wrong thing and, besides, nothing is less funny than the public address announcer who insists on booming forth with a variety of humorous remarks that are appreciated only by himself and a couple of his cronies down at a local bar. The paying public has a right to expect a little better treatment, and what was said earlier about cutting your words to a minimum applies here especially. One mistake, one false word, and you may need police protection in order to leave the park. It has happened.

If there are disputes over an infraction of the rules, do not join in even from the safe vantage point of a booth located several dozen feet in the air. When a misunderstanding occurs, wait until a final decision has been reached by the officials in charge and then give this information, without adornment of any kind, to the waiting public.

Many times at sporting events, you will be asked by some rabid fan or local entrepeneur to work up a little artificial enthusiasm, when the game gets dull or the spectators seem to be merely sitting quietly and not shouting their heads off. Do not attempt any such thing. The public should be the final judge of its reaction to a sporting event, and any effort to pump up enthusiasm is almost certainly doomed to failure.

Basketball.—The rule of saying no more than is absolutely necessary applies with special force at a basketball game. These events are held indoors, and the voice of the public address announcer, louder than the voice of doom, may become very monotonous.

Give the names and positions of the players before the start of the game. Then, as the play proceeds, give the fouls that are called on the various player, together with the number of free throws awarded as a result of the foul. Announce all substitutions and give a recapitulation of the score each time a basket is made. Give the name of the player making the free throws, and naturally, you will tell the kind of foul, whether pushing, tripping, or other infraction of the rules.

In the case of free throws, there is a perfect example of how to handle a microphone so it becomes a help instead of a hindrance. Do not say, "Grabowsky is on the free-throw line preparing to shoot!" The audience can see most of that for themselves. Say, "Grabowsky shooting!" and you will do yeoman's service for the cause of better announcing at athletic events.

Track and Field.—The announcer who lives through an afternoon of track and field games is usually a fit candidate for the madhouse. What happens? In the first place, the games are run off very slowly, with long pauses between moments of feverish activity. Second, a host of scantily clad athletes are scattered like locusts over the field. Periodically someone fires a gun and, while the smoke blows away over the stadium walls, a group of these figures go scampering off in what seems to be a race. They keep paddling along for an indefinite length of time. Finally they collapse upon the grass and are never seen or heard from again. In any case, no one will ever take the trouble to tell you what all this activity means.

Your task at any track and field meet is so to organize your work that the results of each contest reach you in the shortest possible time. If custom prevails, however, the officials in charge will puzzle over the results of each race until, by the time they get to you, the spectators will only remember them vaguely as something that happened during the time of the Second Punic War.

The best plan is to have a couple of runners who will stand breathlessly at the elbows of the officials as events are run off. Then, as a decision is reached, they race toward you with the results written on a sheet of paper.

While one runner is haunting the men in one section of the field, the second man is aligning himself next to the officials at another where the next event is scheduled to be run. In this manner, you can keep a proper relay of information flowing between yourself and the scattered events on the field. As an added help, acquire runners who are aggressive enough to pry information out of the most reluctant officials. The latter are not trying deliberately to keep information from you, with malice aforethought. It is only that, by the time they make up their minds, they have a deep proprietary interest in the results of a race and are reluctant to give them to anyone but the personal representative of the Angel Gabriel himself.

You, for your part, should try to familiarize yourself with the program in advance of your appearance behind the microphone. Then, as events take place in different sections of the field, you can call the attention of the spectators to what is taking place and where and give the names of the participants.

At the conclusion of each contest, give the names of the winners, their school or club affiliation, and the time or the distance involved. Also it might be well if you learned to know some of the more common signs and symbols used in these sports events. For instance, 2:35.3 is read as "two minutes, thirty-five and three-tenths seconds." Keep also within easy reach a chart showing the local, state, or national record in each scheduled event, so that a comparison can be made, should anyone exceed a past performance and a new record be established.

Remember that no record is official until it has been verified by the proper authorities. This means that new records are not really official until approved by the association involved. Go slowly until you have checked with those who are supposed to know. Even when a man wearing a bright yellow badge bustles up to you and announces a new record, stop and ask him whether the record has been checked and pronounced official by the state high school athletic association or some other appropriate authority. Such caution should apply at any sporting event. Do not announce results as official until they really are. You can, of course, announce results as unofficial, but be sure you make the distinction.

Speaking of records, it might be well to insert a word or two about score books. Periodically a manufacturer comes out with a double-duplex, semi-automatic score book to be used at athletic games and contests. It has everything in it but the kitchen sink. If you are wise, you will not use such a contraption without checking it thoroughly. Whether it be for baseball, basketball, or any other sport, it is generally safer to stick to a standard type of score book—one used by professionals. Such books have stood the test of time and are easier to handle than some of the later models.

Learn the professional way to score. The game will be easier to follow, and you will have much less difficulty in reading the results, should it prove necessary to give a recapitulation at the end of the contest.

Races.—Three things must be announced in any race: the

conditions, the participants, and the results. The conditions are anything that those in charge have selected as a prerequisite for that particular race. There may be a motorboat race for Class C runabouts, a horse race for apprentice jockeys, or an automobile race for cars of a certain piston displacement. In addition, any of these races may be for a certain distance and, since all of these conditions were doubtless decided upon a long time before the start of the actual race, it seems fitting to remind all those present what exactly lies in store for them.

If there is an official printed program, it is not always essential that you announce the list of entries in each event. But you should take note of any withdrawals, added entries, or changes in starting position, if this is a factor.

During the race itself, it is sometimes customary to give a running account of what happens, with the announcer calling attention to changes in position throughout the course of the race. Or he may, if he prefers, give the positions of the various contenders as they pass certain stated distances, like the quarter-mile pole in a mile-and-an-eighth horse race. Again, the officials in charge may prefer that the announcer content himself with a bare recital of the conditions, the entries, and the results, as stated previously. In other circumstances, the decision may be left with the announcer himself.

In any case, do not try to give a running account of a race until you have had a little practice or have seen a good many races. A race looks very different when you are calling it than when you are sitting in the stands wondering what is happening to your two-dollar bet.

Granted, but how does one go about getting experience in calling a race? If you have a hankering to do this kind of work, try to get acquainted with some person who already has had a little experience. Ask permission to sit or stand beside him while he calls a race. Then after you have had a chance to see and hear how it is done, call a race yourself under your breath, while your mentor works beside you. In that way, you will be able to judge any relationship between the words you are trying to say and what goes on down upon the track.

Later, at a distance, so as not to interfere with your friend who is acting as coach, make a tape recording and have your teacher listen to what you have done and make suggestions. After you have had a little practice, you can open up on the public.

Remember that unless you are working at a six-day bicycle race, the average contest last only a very few seconds or minutes. You cannot fumble for words. If you do, the whole thing will be over before you can open your mouth.

At most racing events, it is not customary for the public address announcer to give as full a description of the race as a radio announcer would. For the first few times, restrict yourself to the principal changes in position. After that, as you gain more experience, you can give a more complete description of what goes on.

If you are like most beginners, the first time you show up to call a race of any kind, you will be carrying a pair of oversized field glasses. They may prove useful, but if you expect to find them indispensable when calling a long series of races, you are due for a rude surprise.

In a long afternoon of racing, there may be as many as fifty or sixty entries, maybe more. The average field in a horse race includes ten or twelve animals, and there may be as many as six or seven races on an afternoon's program. Unless you are a genius, you will not be able to remember more than a small percentage of these horses, even with the aid of the numbers and the different colors worn by the jockeys. You will have to keep a program handy and refer to it from time to time in order to keep the entries straight.

Operating in this fashion, you very quickly discover that it is physically impossible to focus through glasses on a fast-moving object half a mile or more away, then swing your eyes back to the program and, after that, back to the horses again. The human eye will not accommodate itself to such rapidly changing fields of vision, at least not fast enough.

To keep from going blind, you use the glasses only to

catch such aberrations or departures from the normal — as a mix-up at the starting gate, an accident in the back stretch, or a pair of drunks falling over each other in a corner of the stands. The race itself you follow with the unaided eye.

In many races where mechanical contrivances are a factor —motorboat races, automobile, or motorcycle races—time trials may be held, with the competitors racing against the clock instead of each other. When this happens, your duties are somewhat different. The purpose of the time trials is to determine the class or race in which the contestants are to appear or to determine the positions of the field in the line-up at the start of the race. The fastest man in the time trials takes the "pole" or inside position when the starters line up at the barrier.

During the time trials, your job is to keep track of each man's time and compare it with the fastest time made previously in an effort to add a little sense of competition to the time trials. That feeling is not always present although often the time trials are a crucial part of the race.

Other Sports

Other sports are not too difficult to handle, once you know the basic routine. Learn the sport, check thoroughly, and say no more than is absolutely necessary. These three rules will get you through almost any situation.

As for the rest, there are so many different sports that no living human can hope to be expert at them all. You will find, however, that if you are proficient in one, it will not be too difficult to shift to another.

All of which brings up the old argument: Who makes the better sports announcer? One who knows sports and cannot talk, or one who talks glibly and knows nothing whatever about the subject? It depends upon the individual, but it also means that the person who can talk winds up learning something about sports.

To do a really outstanding job, however, it is advisable that you almost live your subject, a proceeding that demands a real interest in it. Otherwise, surprisingly enough, announcing sports events can become inconceivably dull.

It is not everyone who can whip up a real interest every Friday night in the outcome of the weekly wrestling card at the Elks' Club Auditorium. If you can do it, fine! It not, you may be happier staying home and playing cards with the wife.

CHAPTER SEVEN

OUTDOOR ENTERTAINMENTS

It may seem silly to discuss any such subject as outdoor entertainment when, on the surface, the only difference between an outdoor entertainment and any other kind is that the former is held under the open sky. You will soon discover, however, that those in the outside category fall into a very definite pattern. These entertainments may use athletic events of various kinds. There may be speeches and, to cap the climax, there may be circus or vaudeville acts as spectacular as a herd of elephants.

These three elements may be blended together, in greater or less degree, at picnics, fairs, or celebrations. They are about equal in popularity. But it may be well to understand the highlights of each, in order to know what to expect. There may also be work for a master of ceremonies at an outdoor pageant, but here the job is handled in a somewhat different manner.

Picnics

Picnics are the most informal of all outdoor entertainments. Since this is true, the question might be asked. "What is a master of ceremonies doing at a picnic?"

You are thinking, doubtless, of the small family type of gathering where there is no more use for a master of ceremonies than there is for two tails on a dog. At larger picnics, such as church, school, community, or company picnics, there may be a place for a master of ceremonies, and you may be the one who is called upon to do the job. If you are, you will find it most important to check with the committee beforehand. Since most picnics are disorganized affairs at best, it pays to sit down with the committee in charge of the entertainment and find out if there is really going to be any. Most picnic committees bog down when they get beyond thirty dozen hot dogs and a jar of mustard.

If you are able, you might be prepared to offer a few suggestions. Novelty stunts and races are a good thing to include on the program. Have them for both men and women. If children are present, they should be included in some part of the program, too, and all entertainment should be of the hardy outdoor type. Games and folk dancing serve admirably, and every effort should be made to secure the active participation of everyone concerned. Professional entertainment is sometimes used at large company or community picnics, but the home-grown variety is frequently just as good. Speeches are best if kept at a minimum, and none of them should be too long.

With a program planned or at least the sketch of one prepared, the next step is to check on physical facilities. Some parks have a platform or bandstand built for just such entertainment purposes. Others do not. If there is no such thing as a convenient elevation from which to present your entertainment, one should be provided. It can be built, but the easiest method is to run in a large flat-bed truck and use it as your stage. However, it may be impossible to present such things as tap dancing without first providing a layer of masonite or veneer on the floor of the truck. A stepladder next to the truck can serve as stairs.

Nowadays, it is well nigh impossible to present an outdoor program of any kind without using a sound system. One should be provided for your picnic, but, if no electric outlet is available, a sound system will have to be procured which operates on batteries or, better yet, one that is powered by a small gasoline-driven generator. Since these are rare and rather hard to find, it may be best to change the location of your picnic to a place where electric power is assured.

The sound system may not be absolutely essential, but if you are going to present organized entertainment of any kind, you should have some easy means of corraling the crowd. In considering such means, however, there are a number of things which ought to be kept in mind. At a picnic, city folks especially go slightly berserk. When they reach the open sward, they go charging about and will not submit to the blandishments of anyone trying to carry out an entertainment program. Children, too, often get out of hand.

When that happens, there is no need to stand in front of the microphone and bellow like a bloated bullfrog. Besides, it will do you no good. You can shout at the top of your voice, but if it appears that nothing much is going to be accomplished by shouting, stop immediately. Your red-faced roaring will only spoil the fun for everybody else. Stay relaxed!

Go ahead with your planned program and ignore those who are endangering life and limb in other sections of the park. When they get tired of what they are doing, they may come back and join the more docile lambs under your control.

If not, forget it. Find a pleasant spot under a tree and go to sleep. The behavior of people at picnics is one of the unalterable laws of life, and there is no need for you to worry yourself into an early grave trying to change it.

Celebrations

There are a number of names under which the local community-wide celebration or festival can disguise itself. Some of these festivities are known as Rutabaga Days, Cranberry Days, and Watermelon Days. Sometimes the occasion may be known as a harvest festival. At others, it may be called Commercial Day, Community Day, or Field Day. It may be any occasion when the local citizenry band together to present a celebration to attract people to the town, in the hope that they may come back to do business at a later date.

In the smaller towns, a baseball game may be the leading feature of the attraction. In the morning there may be a number of activities for the children—races, contests, and games. Around noon, usually about eleven o'clock, there may be a street parade, with prizes offered for the various floats. In the afternoon, if anything is offered besides the standard athletic contest, there may be a vaudeville program, followed by an address from some visiting celebrity. In the evening, the day may be brought to a conclusion by a fireworks display or an outdoor stage performance, or there may be a street dance or a dance held in the schoolhouse or other hall. In between times, a band concert may be thrown in by local musicians or by those who may have wandered over from a neighboring community.

As far as disorganization goes, the entertainment may be only one step above a picnic. On the other hand, with communities that have been doing this sort of thing for years, the proceedings may be run with a smoothness and efficiency that would do credit to a Broadway showman.

It is well, at the outset, to suggest that more than one man be used as master of ceremonies. If you have the constitution of a horse, you may be able to go the entire day without wearing out, but it is extremely difficult to keep your freshness after you have been shouting into a microphone for two or three hours, particularly if—as so often happens—the celebration is staged in the middle of a hot and dusty street.

A good idea is to divide the program into three parts, with one man each handling the morning, afternoon, and evening sessions. If there is a shortage of masters of ceremonies, the man from the morning can serve during the evening as this section of the entertainment is generally the simplest of the lot. Besides, he will have had an opportunity to refresh himself.

The races in the morning can be handled as suggested for the picnic, but there are a number of other points which ought to be considered. At events of this kind, there never seem to be enough judges. There is always a dispute over who won the three-legged race, or something of the sort. Mistakes are made, and there is a good deal of unhappiness. As a result, the races do not go very far toward fostering good will— which was the announced purpose of the celebration.

Try to have the committee appoint as many judges as there are going to be prize winners in each race. That is, if there are to be three prize winners and three prizes are to be awarded, select three judges. Then each judge is responsible for picking only one winner and can keep an eye on him during the confusion. To make doubly sure that there are no mistakes, each judge should corral his individual prize winner at the conclusion of each race and escort him to the judge's stand, where the awards are made. In this way and in this way only, can you be certain that the right person is going to get the right prize. Do not wait until the last minute to appoint your judges. Get them earlier, before the day of the race, and recruit hardy souls who are willing to remain until the whole thing is over.

There should also be a couple of starters to make sure that each race is started properly.

If precautions of a similar sort are not taken, there is certain to be a disagreement of some kind, with an irate mother storming up to the judge's stand and complaining that her little Johnny did not get the prize to which he was entitled. Indeed, there have been instances of more aggressive youngsters crowding up to the judge's stand to claim prizes that rightfully belonged to another and a shyer child.

It is certain, if the prizes are worth while, that there is bound to be an unmanageable crush of youngsters. Make sure that your committee plans to have a policeman present—as much for the moral effect as anything—or the purpose of your entire program may evaporate in the unhappiness of a few disgruntled prize-winners.

The afternoon session of a community celebration may take a variety of forms, depending upon the town. In smaller communities, a platform may be erected at a principal street intersection and the program given there. Again, the program may be presented at a ball park, at a community bandstand, or in front of the grandstand at the local fairgrounds.

However it is done, you will undoubtedly be faced with a great diversity of material, both amateur and professional. You will have to use good judgment in combining the whole, or you may wind up with a hodgepodge of no particular value to anyone.

Especially will you have to check those acts which use special equipment, rigging, or tables and chairs. If you get into difficulties on an open platform in a public square, there is very little that you or anyone else can do to save the situation.

Since, in many cases, the crowd will be standing, try to use only those acts which are short and have a good deal of action. Circus acts are best—trained dogs and ponies, unicycle acts, or acrobats, although other types may be used as well— tap dancers, instrumentalists, or folk singers and dancers. The last-named should be groups rather than individual soloists, although here again the exception may only serve to prove the rule.

Professional acts are obtained from theatrical booking offices in the larger cities or from radio stations which make a business of handling such entertainment. Unless the committee buying professional acts has an unusually large budget, patronize those offices which are nearer home. Otherwise, transportation charges for bringing the entertainers a long distance will eat up all the fund and quality will suffer as a result. When buying acts, it is wisest to get the best that the market affords, for good entertainment can make up for any deficiencies that may exist in other parts of the program.

The visiting speaker at these affairs is generally some political figure on a fence-mending tour and, unless the situation is a bit unusual, it will not fall to the lot of the regular master of ceremonies to make his introduction. Instead, that task will fall to some local luminary anxious to bask in the glory of the great one, and you will introduce him. Rather than regard such treatment as a slight, you will find, after a long and arduous program, that it merely gives you welcome relief and a better opportunity to rest your aching back and feet.

There is one thing you will need at occasions of this kind, and that is a liberal supply of patience. You will be expected to make all kinds of service announcements—announcements for lost children, the winners in the various contests, the names of merchants who donated prizes, the winners of the various prizes donated in the street parade, and the like. You will also be expected to "plug" the upcoming attractions, like the dance at night, in order to get a good crowd.

These announcements will have to be made at everyone else's convenience and not your own and, although it is still advisable to use discretion, sorting out those which are essential from those which are merely a nuisance.

Type up several copies of the order of program or have them mimeographed. Give the approximate starting time of each number or act and have these schedules posted where the speakers or entertainers have ready access to them. Make a note at the top of the schedule to the effect that the times given are only approximate and that each person is responsible for seeing to it that he gets to the platform on time. Unless you do this when you have a lot of stray acts or people who have never worked together before, you will be driven to distraction trying to answer questions, and your own work will suffer as a result. By posting the schedule, you answer many questions before they are asked, since most performers will want to know when they appear. You can thus restrict yourself to those which are really important.

This suggestion again points to the importance of discussing the entire program with the committee in charge. As the master of ceremonies, you are always one of the more conspicuous parts of the entertainment and people naturally gravitate to you with questions. By knowing the answers, or most of them, you can better help the cause along or, if you do not know the answers, you should at least know the name of the person to whom the questioner can be referred. In this way, you can get him out of your hair.

Actually, with the exception of the changed background, there is nothing in this matter of celebrations which has not been discussed before. Try to find the most salable feature in each act and present it in such a way that it seems as attractive as possible.

The rest of the time you attempt to preserve an even disposition under conditions that can prove very trying indeed. For instance, at the average outdoor show, if the weather looks the least bit stormy, dozens of people will come to you and ask if you think it is going to rain. In answering this profound question, you point a finger toward heaven and intone piously, "God alone knows!" The pest will look at you fearfully, then edge quietly away.

Outdoor Announcements

From the foregoing, you can see that the material which you are expected to introduce at an outdoor celebration is so varied that it is almost impossible to give sample announcements. Nevertheless, there are some activities which are so typical that a few examples might be given.

Generally speaking, it is much less desirable to indulge in humor or fancy phrases than it is indoors because the crowd is so huge and the distractions so many that such subtleties are lost. Stick to broad effects and concentrate on being understood rather than anything else.

Since you are expected to give credit to the sponsoring organization for their perspicacity in arranging such a noteworthy event, you might as well include it in the opening introduction. A fair example might go like this:

Good afternoon, ladies and gentlemen! Welcome to our third annual celebration of Rutabaga Days, staged under the sponsorship of the Clinker Falls' Booster Club. We are happy to have so many of you and we hope that you are all thoroughly enjoying yourselves. This afternoon, we have a star-studded program for your entertainment but, before we begin, I'm sure that we've all enjoyed the preliminary concert presented by the Municipal Band from Binghamton Center. The band played this afternoon under its regular director, Mr. Ernest Hotchkiss. Mr. Hotchkiss, on behalf of your musicians, take a bow for your contribution to this afternoon's program.

The master of ceremonies secures a round of applause for the Binghamton Band, then quickly goes on to introduce the first number. Later, after the show is well under way, he might introduce a representative of the Booster Club who can thank those present for their support. This can be done in a manner somewhat like the following:

As I told you earlier, our program today has been produced under the sponsorship of the Clinker Falls' Booster Club. We are now to hear briefly from the organization in the person of its president, Mr. Tom Collins, who, with his committees, has done so much to make their Rutabaga Days an outstanding success. Mr. Collins:

Mr. Collins then goes on to thank those present for their attendance and to make such statements of appreciation as he considers necessary for the work of his committees. If there is any unusual announcement in connection with Rutabaga Days, such as a record number of visitors from out of town, that fact can be given as a sort of climax to Mr. Collins' talk, thus insuring that he will sit down to at least a smattering of applause. Such talks should naturally be kept as brief as possible.

Assume now that the first number on the program is a tap dance by a group of very young ladies from a local dancing school. Picking up from the opening, your introduction might go as follows:

As an opening bit of color on our program today, we present a chorus of tap dancers from the primary class at the Clinker Falls Dancing Academy. Accompanied by Miss Myrtle Beck, here they are with— The Tiny Town Parade!

Incidentally, on occasions similar to this, it is well to have someone check up on the piano. On these programs, where the entertainment is presented out of doors, the piano provided is most likely to be some broken down old upright that has been rescued from behind the furnace in a church basement. The trip to the platform has done it no good either; it is sadly out of tune and one or two keys are apt to be dead. Mention these facts to someone in charge of the program, or you will have to listen to an endless amount of complaining from those who are expected to play the thing. Also, some pianos are tuned differently from the instruments which they are expected to accompany but, when you meet a situation like this, there is very little you can do about it except to try and keep from losing your mind.

To get back to our introductions, mention was made earlier of the situation in which you introduce the person who will, in turn, introduce the person who is to be the principal speaker of the day. It can be done in the following manner:

We have now reached the principal part of our program. To introduce our speaker for the day, here is Mr. Henry W. Wadsworth, local chairman for the Republocrat Central Committee. Mr. Wadsworth.

Service announcements or plugs for upcoming attractions such as the dance that night are best if given before the end of the program. Otherwise, you might wind up delivering them to the backs of your departing audience. Try to intersperse them in an earlier part of the program. Here is a sample plug:

Don't forget the dance tonight at the high school gymnasium. Tickets are only a dollar and a half a couple. Music is being provided by Heinie Wentworth and His Alsatian German Band. There will be both modern and old-time dancing from nine until one. Tickets are only a dollar and a half a couple, remember, and they can be purchased at the high school gymnasium tonight or at Carpenter's Music, 110 Clinker Boulevard.

Fairs

Most often, a professional master of ceremonies who comes to town with a traveling troupe will officiate at your local fair, but there are enough occasions when a home-town product may be asked to serve to make it worth while going into the subject.

At any fair, there are really two separate and distinct types of programs—the afternoon show and the one in the evening. The afternoon program is most often a combination of "free acts" and racing; the evening performance is a revue spiced by circus acts and climaxed with a fireworks display. You may be asked to appear only at one section of the entertainment, since it is customary, especially during the afternoon, to have more than one master of ceremonies.

All of which brings up another subject: switching the microphone from one announcer to another. During the course of a long, hot afternoon, it can get very monotonous if the announcers go through an Alphonse-and-Gaston routine every time they exchange places.

The first announcer comes on "cold." He introduces the next man, with just enough information for the audience to understand who he is. Then, when the microphone is finally turned back to the original announcer who appeared without benefit of any announcement, the man preceding says a few words about him.

Thereafter, the changes are made in the simplest possible manner. For example: "Here's your track-side announcer!" or "Here's the master of ceremonies for your free-acts program!" If the men can see each other, verbal exchanges may not be needed. Hand signals will be enough.

Incidentally, the so-called free acts are not really free. They used to be, in the days of the old street and community fairs, when they were performed on an open street. The term is a holdover from earlier times and refers nowadays to any act presented in front of the grandstand as part of the afternoon program at a fair. In carnivals, when some man stands on his ear atop a hundred-and-fifty-foot pole, merely to attract a crowd—and no admission is paid—that is a free act, of the pure and unsullied sort. The others are dubbed free by courtesy only.

Your duties as racing announcer will be confined to announcing the starters in each race, together with the names of the drivers or jockeys as the case may be. With running races, the weights are given, and, if pari-mutuel betting is permitted, the odds are announced, provided this work is not done by the handicapper or other person directly connected with the pari-mutuel set-up.

In this connection, it might be said that pari-mutuel betting is perfectly legal, operating under the laws of the various states. A portion of the money is returned to the state in the form of taxes, a portion goes to the institution operating the track, and the rest is apportioned out among the public under a system that is very difficult to understand but perfectly honest in every way. Therefore when you announce odds that are part of the pari-mutuel system of betting, regardless of how you may feel about the subject personally, you are engaged in an activity that has honorable auspices and that has been made specifically legal under the laws of your own state.

Fairs are presumed to be agricultural exhibitions. Despite the races, the carnival attractions, and the general circus-like atmosphere, the promotion of agriculture through exhibits, demonstrations, and contests is their principal reason for being. Consequently state legislators consider it legitimate to take money that might be bet anyway and divert a portion of it into the promotion of better farming and livestock practices.

At least that is the theory. In actual practice, most of the money comes from the entertainment features on the program and fair managements place a great deal of emphasis upon them. The fair secretary or chief member of the local fair board is usually the man who is in charge of the grandstand program. The various other duties, such as the supervision of the livestock and poultry exhibits, are placed in the hands of others who may work only as part-time employees of the organization.

The racing program is normally under the direct management of a professional racing superintendent, who is hired for that specific purpose. Most of these men are very capable, and you will find it a joy to work with them. They are firm in the dispatch of their duties and return to the same fair year after year.

The conditions of a race may be announced in the following manner: "The second race of the afternoon—the Governor's special! For 2:17 trotters, five years old and over, owner-trained and driven! Purse, $500." The terms, "2:17 trotter," "five years old and over" and "owner-trained and driven" all refer to the conditions of the race. In this instance, the race is for trotters that regularly cover a mile in two minutes and seventeen seconds and are trained and driven by their owners instead of a hired driver; the inference being that local drivers would be more evenly matched than would be true if part of them were local and the rest from out of town.

Announcement of the starters is made as the participants in the race come upon the track for the initial parade in front of the grandstand. If horses are "scratched"—that is to say, withdrawn from the race—give this information, together with any other deviations there might be from the official program.

This information will be relayed to you by the track steward, who is in communication with your post by portable telephone. At least that is the way it usually is. If you are working under conditions that are fairly primitive—and they still exist—the information may be brought to you by a small boy, who races breathlessly between the speed barns and your post atop the grandstand or wherever it is you are located.

In announcing the list of horses and riders or drivers, always start from the pole position—the position of the horse nearest the rail or inside—and read out. Remember that in harness races, which are customarily run in three heats, the horses change position in each heat, with the winner of the preceding heat taking the pole position, the number two horse the second position, and so on out.

Results are announced when made official by the judges and, in the event of a photo finish, it may take a moment or two for the winners of the race to be established. Photo finishes occur when two or more horses reach the finish line so closely bunched that it is difficult to detect the winner with the naked eye. A camera, located high in the grandstand, takes a picture of the finish. This photograph is used in determining the winner.

If you have given a running account of the race, you will have to announce the unofficial results, which should later be either changed or confirmed in accordance with the decision of the judges. Say, "I will now give you the official results of the second race," or "The previous results are now official."

The free acts at an afternoon fair program consist mainly of acrobatic turns, variety numbers, and thrill acts. These numbers appear on the free acts platform in front of the grandstand, on the infield—the large oval area inside the track—or on the track itself. They are sandwiched in between the races—which explains why it is necessary to switch back and forth from one announcer to another.

At this point, it may be well to remind you of one of your principal responsibilities. Never, as a public address announcer, whether it be at a fair or anywhere else, are you supposed to wander very far from the scene. It will not do, for instance, to have the racing announcer switch the program over to you at the free acts' platform, only to discover that you are nowhere to be found. You cannot wander off searching for ice cream cones, joke with your fellow entertainers, or idly dream. One missed cue is likely to prove very embarrassing, so you must tend strictly to business. Besides, there may be an emergency or an accident, and your services may be required instantly. In such cases, you would doubtless prefer to be at hand.

This close attention to business can get very wearing, but after all you are getting paid for it. If you are doing the announcing on any job as exacting as a fair, it is presumed you are good enough to get at least some returns on your services.

When it comes to the free acts, try to interview personally a leading member in each act, to find out if there is any special material which must be included in their announcement. Most of these performers have had a great deal of experience and often will be able to give you ideas, used before, which will enable you to do a better-than-average job of making an introduction.

Then, too, many circus or thrill acts require additional announcing during the course of their performance. There may be some trick or principal feat which must be highlighted by an additional word from the announcer. At an appropriate moment, you may be expected to say over the microphone, "Ladies and gentlemen, from her perch one hundred and eighteen feet in the air, Miss Eileen now does the rhumba."

Strangely enough, you will discover that the principal members of many acts are not those who appear in front of the public. Do not be surprised if some older person, with knotted muscles and a mahogany-colored face, comes to tell you what is required in the way of special announcing. Many times, these people really own the acts, and the bright little cherubs who appear before the public merely work for them.

Other acts have what is known as a semi-finish. Arabian tumblers may build their act to a final whirl, then run off stage as though their performance were concluded. Then, as the applause swells to its height, they run out again and apparently start all over. Semi-finishes are not encores. They are planned as a part of the act. They are designed to gain extra applause for a trick or a feature which might not be appreciated in its original setting.

Ordinarily a master of ceremonies will not make an appearance during a semi-finish but will allow the act to worry along with its own applause-making machinery. The leaders of most acts will warn you when they have a semi-finish, thus implying that you are to stay out of the way until the act is really over.

Often at fair shows, during the afternoon program, the music will be played by a local band, which, for all its virtues, is not too well acquainted with the requirements of the different acts. You may be asked to watch for a specific cue— a change in tempo or a change in tune—or complete silence may be requested while members of an act prepare for an especially difficult trick. When that happens, your job is to stand by the band director as a double check to see that he does not miss his cue. For the moment you will have to violate the rule of staying out of sight unless there is a specific demand for your services.

How many times have you been at a performance during which the master of ceremonies or some other member of the troupe played around in full view of the audience? You will not follow this practice if you wish to adopt a fully professional attitude toward your work. Keep your mind on your business and do not detract from the performance by engaging in antics or horseplay in full view of the audience.

The night show is like a revue. On the fair platform, because of its greater distances, you will have to move faster or you will never get where you are going.

At night shows you are most likely to meet with one of those unfriendly pauses that occur while a "high act" has its equipment set up behind you. During these pauses, work in special announcements or tell one of your more potent extensible stories. If you are wise, you will not attempt to tell an extensible story during the afternoon program. There are too many distractions. There are not many masters of ceremonies who can compete too successfully with a ferris wheel and the high-pitched bleating of a calliope.

The climax of the night show is the fireworks display. You can add a great deal to this part of the program by learning about some of the more elaborate displays and explaining what they are to the audience. Almost everyone is familiar with "Niagara Falls." But you may be able to get a little extra applause for the display if you give the names of some of the more elaborate set pieces or some of the rockets or bombs which are being exploded.

At all professional shows, you can get this information from the man in charge. He will doubtless give you a routine sheet of the entire exhibit. With care, you will be able to follow it quite easily as the various fireworks are displayed. The man in charge can generally be located in a little tent somewhere at the back of the infield.

It can be unnerving at times to step before a fair audience and discover that it extends about a block on either side of you. Those thousands of people, however, are no different from any others. They laugh at the same jokes and react in much the same way as any other audience.

For maximum effectiveness, it is desirable that you speak a trifle more slowly than usual, but only a trifle. Even with the microphone, you must make a special effort to see that your words are understood in the remotest reaches of the grandstand. Enunciate clearly and on windy days be more careful than ever because the wind has a tendency to distort whatever you say. Exaggeration is not needed, but reasonable care should be used.

If the wind can be heard over the microphone in a kind of continuous whistle, tie a handkerchief over it. Or the technician in charge may supply you with a little sock, either of cloth or pliofilm, to cut down the whistling of the wind.

At the same time, try to keep in mind that, before so large an audience, small effects are no good. If you are going to gesture, make the gesture big or, at least, good-sized. There is no use in trying to succeed with the kind of work that might be effective in a night club. You will have to project, and that means making sure that every last thing you say or do is plainly understood by those who are seated a maximum distance from you.

Pageants

Every once in a while, there is a revival of interest in the subject of pageants, although nowadays the old-time pageant may be found masquerading under some such name as "sociodrama." Whatever you choose to call it, the full-fledged master of ceremonies should be familiar with what is expected of him when he is asked to say a few well-chosen words at one of these affairs.

Strictly speaking, at most pageants, the master of ceremonies will not function as one. He will be a narrator, one who reads from a script while the deathless drama is enaced upon a nearby verdant hillside. Accordingly he will be expected to use his most melodious tones and to read the script with unction and style.

Since most pageants are staged with a minimum of rehearsal, you will do well to have more than a vague notion of what the script is all about, or you may wind up describing the landing of the Pilgrims at Plymouth Rock while an Indian massacre is taking place. As you plod through the script at rehearsal, make added marginal notes where they seem to be needed, and you can follow these during the performance.

Occasionally at pageants, too, if things run true to form, you will have to pause while the action catches up with you. Delays of some sort are almost inevitable. When they occur, maintain a spirit of detached calm and, when the situation has righted itself, go on about your business.

Drawings and Lotteries

At many fairs or outdoor performances, there will be a drawing or lottery. A car is given away or some other award is made in the interest of boosting attendance.

In some states, lotteries are illegal. In others, they are encouraged. They are permissible at some types of entertainment and not at others. It is a good idea for you to know all such facts, or you may wind up in the local jail. Usually, of course, if the enterprise is being managed by responsible people, you can be assured that everything is all right.

As a rule, those in charge are quite happy if someone else takes the job of conducting the lottery off their hands. In the search for a likely victim, their glance will most often fall on the master of ceremonies. When it does, you should have more than a vague idea of what is expected of you.

First of all, it is absolutely essential that you avoid even the appearance of dishonesty. For every prize winner, there may be several thousand who are disappointed. Therefore you must be very careful as to how you conduct the drawing, or several hundred of these people may descend on you or your sponsors. Use caution!

Actually there are only two things which have to be remembered. Announce plainly the conditions under which the drawing is to be conducted, and then conduct it in such a manner that it is obviously fair. Beyond that, you need have few worries.

When numbered tickets are used, the holder must be on the grounds or in the grandstand to win. It may be necessary to draw several numbers before a winner is found. When names and addresses are written on the tickets, the first one drawn is ordinarily the winner. If several prizes are awarded, it is best to start with the minor prizes and work up to the grand climax—the awarding of the trip to Europe, the automobile, or the electric range with the built-in percolator.

At small fairs, three judges can be picked from the audience or three well-known citizens can be asked to serve. It is the duty of two of the judges to operate the "squirrel cage" in which the tickets are mixed. One judge turns the crank, while the second one opens the door through which the tickets are withdrawn. A child, selected from the audience, makes the drawing. The child hands the ticket to the third judge who, in plain view of the audience, verifies the number and then hands it on to the master of ceremonies, who reads it over the microphone.

A reasonable amount of time should be given prize winners to reach the stage, and when each number is announced, it should be repeated at least twice and oftener, if requested.

Sometimes tricky procedures are used when drawing numbers from the cage. Every other number is declared a winner or a stated number of tickets, like ten or fifteen, may be drawn from the cage before pay dirt is reached. However, such methods of drawing seem unnecessarily cumbersome and should not be used unless requested by the men in charge. Whatever method is used, each time a ticket is withdrawn, the squirrel cage should be closed and the machine revolved, thus mixing the tickets, before another number is withdrawn.

When winners are selected, they should be introduced from the stage. Their names should be given and, should it prove interesting, their addresses or their occupations. If a winner is from out of town, that fact also should be given some prominence.

The procedure outlined here may seem a bit awkward, but it has been used successfully countless times, and no one conducting a drawing along these lines has even been slain by a disappointed ticket holder or met with violence of any kind.

There really is no end to the number of outdoor entertainments at which a master of ceremonies may be asked to show his wares. There are dog and cattle shows. There are rodeos. There are even such weird and wonderful manifestations of sport as gymkhanas, where horses and men and women compete and where you are apt to run into such odd things as a Gretna Green contest.

When you meet something unfamiliar, remember the rules. Ask a multitude of questions beforehand, or have someone at hand to prompt you in the event that you start going wrong while the exhibit is under way. Be sure to tell your expert to stay close at hand. While the show is on, you are literally chained to the microphone. You cannot wander off in search of him while he swaps stories with neighbors or friends. Therefore, make sure that your guest expert stays where you can reach him when needed. Other than that, you need have few worries about an outdoor entertainment.

CHAPTER EIGHT

MASTER OF CEREMONIES AS ENTERTAINER

Some folks never consider a master of ceremonies as very entertaining under any circumstances. You might as well face that fact right at the beginning. Some of them have even expressed the opinion that all masters of ceremonies should be shot. Unless you are unduly thin-skinned, however, you can afford to ignore such malcontents and go about your business as though nothing were amiss.

The reason behind such an attitude is that the master of ceremonies is a hybrid. He falls into a different niche. He is half actor, half public speaker. As a result, he may arouse the animosity of those who feel that he ought to be either one or the other.

However, if you are reasonably adept at your work, this attitude need not bother you too much. You will soon discover that there are many jobs you can fill better than those who are experienced in only one of the two fields.

Audience Participation Shows

It would seem that there have been enough audience participation shows on radio or television for everyone to know how they function. However, there are a few points which ought to be thoroughly covered for the benefit of the master of ceremonies who has never handled them.

In the first place, a quiz or audience participation show is a program in which the general public participates on a more or less extemporaneous basis, with little or no coaching beforehand. This means that the master of ceremonies may be the only person in the show who really knows what is happening. He must be extra familiar with what he proposes to do, or the program may die of its own weight.

It would seem quite simple to stand up before an audience with a pack of cards in your hands, on which are written a series of questions and answers. For that is what the average audience participation show is—a quiz. If you do no more than this, however, you are headed for trouble. There are pitfalls in any quiz show, and you should have some idea of what they are before you start.

Inevitably you will discover that it is not possible to get by with a simple quiz, in which the contestant is asked a single question, and then he either sits down or takes home the mink-lined refrigerator. There has to be a "gimmick," consisting of a series of questions in ascending interest or some other handicap or a contest-within-a-contest, to make it more interesting.

If you are operating on the local level and appearing before your own club or organization, the best way is frankly to imitate one of the better-known quiz shows or give it minor variations that might make it more palatable to your audience.

If, however, you do decide to go ahead with a show of your own, you must be careful to do it in such a way that no hidden jokers are present. For example, if you plan a show in which you decide to double the value of the prize each time the contestant successfully answers the question, you must decide beforehand where the doubling is going to end or the contestant may go home owning the local schoolhouse and the scalp of the master of ceremonies as well.

Before you stage any quiz, sit down with one or two advisers and go over the program to its ultimate conclusion. Find out what happens if the contestant successfully answers every question and wins the highest prize you have to offer. What happens to those who do not win? Is the contest fair? Will it repay in entertainment value for the amount of time and energy expended?

You had better work out the answers to these questions ahead of time, or you are going to be painfully surprised when you get before an audience and find that things are going wrong. If the idea is not absolutely guaranteed foolproof, you had better not use it.

Another thing: Have some of your advisers with you when the show is going on. They can aid in making decisions by a nod or a shake of the head, when it appears that you are heading for trouble. They can even pass you written notes, if need be. Make sure that such notes are legibly written, or you may wind up worse off than ever because you divide your energies in trying to decipher the note. By having people help you, you are relieved of some of the responsibility. Then, if things go wrong, you will not have to take all the blame yourself, and there will be a court of law to which you can appeal after the program is over.

Here are some of the things which have to be considered when you are dealing with the public on a quiz. What happens if the program ends in a tie? What happens if a single contestant runs off with all the prizes? All of these possibilities must be considered before you ever step in front of an audience. Afterward you can start concentrating on what it takes to make a good performance.

A quiz show, regardless of the format, is held together by one thing alone, and that is tempo. Each question is normally a self-contained unit. Interest can last only so long. It is essential, therefore, that you leap into the next question before the audience has time to discover that there is really nothing which holds the structure together. Speed does not mean that you have to get rattled or lose your self-possession. But it does mean that, once started, you have to keep going.

Selecting the right kind of questions is of prime importance. Unless some special purpose is being served, questions of a broad general interest are best. If not, special interest questions can be used. For instance, if the quiz is being used to provide entertainment at the annual meeting of the Red Cross, the questions might be built around some phase of the work of the Red Cross.

Try to have a good cross section of questions. Have them in varying degrees of difficulty. Then, when someone has an unusual amount of trouble in trying to figure out an answer, ease up on the next question or give him a slightly more concise clue. After you have asked the question, repeat it, if necessary, or if the contestant continues to fumble for an answer, give him a clue.

When conducting a quiz in person, before a club or organization, it is not so important to keep the show alive with chatter as it is on the radio or in television, but there is no profit in letting it fall apart either. Try to keep going with enough running comment to maintain the interest of your audience without, at the same time, destroying the concentration, if any, of your contestant.

If you have difficulty thinking of subjects for such chatter, make notes ahead of time on the weather, impending holidays, or any thing else and clip the notes where you can refer to them when needed.

Decide also exactly how much time will be allotted to each contestant to answer a question. Keep rigidly to this schedule and have someone, designated a judge, signal when the allotted time has elapsed. An audible signal, such as a whistle or a bell, is best.

Type your questions on four-by-six-inch cards. Type both the question and the answer on a single card. Along with the answer, type additional information that might serve to verify the correctness of the answer in the minds of the audience, such as, "That's right! The answer is Alcatraz, the well-known prison on the rock in San Francisco Bay!" On each card also, type a number of clues or other comments that might be used in the event that your contestant has difficulty in thinking of the answer.

Have a rack—a music rack will do—on which you can place your questions, graded, in three piles, with the hardest questions on the left, the easiest on the right, and those of medium difficulty in the middle. If you have an assistant, he or she can hand you the proper-type question, but under average conditions you will have to make these decisions for yourself. It will pay you, therefore, to have your questions arranged in such a way that you can pick and choose without having to fumble or make your indecision too obvious to the audience.

The purpose of such an arrangement is to equalize the difficulties of the contest. If a contestant misses a question, ease up a little on the next one, or if it appears that a contestant is having too easy a time of it, make the next question one of increasing difficulty.

If you adopt a quiz where the contestants answer a series of questions in the same category, you will not be able to use the method outlined above. But it will be well to perfect some arrangement by which the quiz master has some control over the quality of the questions, or you may find yourself faced with a situation in which nobody can answer the questions, and that is a development too horrible to contemplate. You avoid that possibility by having on your rack a number of questions which anyone can answer, even if he is barely able to speak a simple English sentence.

Arrange on your rack also a sheet or card on which are typed a number of hints or suggestions on questions to be asked each contestant before the contest gets under way. With enough of these, you can avoid having your get-acquainted or warm-up questions follow too monotonous a pattern.

When working in this part of your program, do not use questions which your contestant can answer with a simple "yes" or "no." Pick questions designed to make your contestant feel at ease by talking about himself. Not only will you get a greater assortment of answers when you use this method, but any initial nervousness on the part of your contestant is more likely to disappear.

Humor is acceptable in the quiz show, but it rarely should be inserted at the expense of the contestant. Stories, if used, should be kept rather short. One or two-line gags are best. But here again you may have to use your own judgment and vary the pattern, depending on conditions.

There are other types of audience participation shows, most of them modeled after the old game of "Truth and Consequences." But the quiz is the most reliable and the easiest to do. Should you decide to present a different show, use the same pattern suggested for the quiz. Follow the outline until you discover how it all comes out. Use an established pattern or make sure that the one you originate is one hundred per cent foolproof. When you are dealing with the public, it does not pay to make too many mistakes. You are either right, or you are completely wrong.

Of necessity, much of your work in the audience quiz show will be completely spontaneous, but a study of the following text may give you a more concrete idea of the form, content and length of the average quiz show dialogue:

EMCEE: Here comes another likely looking prospect. Let's hope he wins some of this filthy lucre we're distributing this evening. What did you say your name was?

GUEST: Smith.

EMCEE: Is that your right name, or are you really in disguise?

GUEST: That's my right name.

EMCEE: I guess I'm left with it then. What's your first name?

GUEST: Roger.

EMCEE: What do you do, Roger?

GUEST: I'm a welder.

EMCEE: A what-er?

GUEST: A welder.

EMCEE: Let's skip the rest of it. We could go around indefinitely, and I hardly think it would be worth while. Where do you do this alleged welding of yours?

GUEST: At the Johnson Plumbing Shop.

EMCEE: Smi'h and Johnson. Those names are too common. Are you sure you're not named Poniatovski or something of the sort?

GUEST: No.

EMCEE: What will you do with all this money—if you win any?

GUEST: Spend it.

EMCEE: That's the first honest answer we've had here tonight. All right! You've chosen "Names of Famous Buildings" as your category. Ready? Here's your first question and, remember, you get "Double Your Dollars" for every correct answer. What is the name of the famous building in Rome where the early Christians were martyred?

GUEST: The Colosseum.

EMCEE: Right! Now, remember, you "Double Your Dollars." You have one dollar. Answer the next question correctly and you get two. What was the famous building in London where Anne Boleyn was imprisoned before she was beheaded? (THE GUEST FAILS TO ANSWER.) You'll remember that Anne Boleyn was one of the wives of Henry the VIII who had quite a few of them.

GUEST: The Tower of London.

EMCEE: Right again. You're doing famously, Mr. Smith—if that's your name. You've got two dollars. Are you ready for four? This is the world renowned museum in Paris where many famous paintings are hanging, among them the Mona Lisa. What is the name of this building?

GUEST: I know the name, but I can't think of it.

EMCEE: It's a French name, of course, and it has an extra syllable on the end which we don't ordinarily pronounce.

GUEST: The Louvre?

EMCEE: Well, is it or isn't it?

GUEST: I'll say The Louvre.

EMCEE: And you'd be absolutely right! You've won four dollars, Mr. Smith, and the right to compete in the grand sweepstakes—where you may win a trip to Hodgkins Corners and a hand engraved faucet for your kitchen sink.

The Style Revue

Style revues are very prevalent at certain seasons of the year, and they provide an opportunity for the mistress of ceremonies to come into her own. They are sometimes called fashion shows, and they are held in stores, at clubs, at luncheons, or to entertain the ladies at conventions while the male half of the contingent are off on what are presumed to be weightier concerns.

It is exceptional when a style revue has more than cursory rehearsals. It is well, therefore, to take steps to prevent those unfortunate incidents which are likely to occur.

Backstage should be posted an iron-clad order in which the models are to be seen on the stage. By making sure that everyone adheres to this schedule, you make less certain the possibility that someone will appear wearing a mink coat while you are describing the revealing features of the latest swim suit.

If the models double—that is, change from one costume to another—it is most important for you to make sure that there is sufficient time for the changes. Such precautions may not be vital in an amateur revue, where there is generally a model for every costume. But if a model appears in more than one costume, make sure that there is enough time for the change, or you may be left high and dry on a vacant stage while the missing model, offstage, struggles out of one costume and into another.

In some places, especially in the larger cities, the continuity for the style revue will be written for you by a buyer or other person connected with the store or group of stores which are furnishing the costumes. At other times, you may have to do the work yourself.

Go to the department head or store owner and ask questions. You will have to ask many of them because the person you see, even though he purchased the garment himself and hopes to sell it at a profit, will not be able to describe it except in the vaguest terms. He (or she) will hold it up on a hanger and say, "Look! See! Isn't it lovely?", and you will have to take it from there.

Besides, so much nonsense has grown up around the writing of fashion copy that the average merchant is apt to hold up his hands in horror when asked to write any part of it. He will be glad to leave it to you.

When you start writing copy, you will have to know whether the dress is by a recognized manufacturer, what the material is, what the style features of the garment are and whether they are in the current mode or whether they are a departure from it. If accessories, like hats, bags and shoes, are important, they should likewise be included in the commentary.

As for decorative flourishes in the copy, any decision you make in this regard will have to be yours. Make it as rapturous as you like, if you think you can get away with it. On the other hand, if you are the average woman, you may do better if you keep your copy fairly matter of fact, with only a dash of purple prose here and there to add to the effect and to prove to the waiting world that you can do it.

Write it out if you wish, but you may prefer to speak from notes. Either way, type your material on three-by-five cards and read or glance at these from time to time as you stand at the microphone. Shuffle each card under the others as you complete the description of any individual costume in the parade.

Remember, too, that most merchants hate style shows and hate them heartily. Costumes are ruined by make-up, by fast changes, and by hasty or inexpert alterations. Invariably at the end of each revue, those responsible for furnishing the costumes will be heard loudly declaring that they never again will engage in such an enterprise.

Do not be surprised, therefore, when one of these individuals takes you aside after it is all over and entertains you with a bitter recital of his woes. Take it in stride, secure in the knowledge that the next time the complainer will probably do it all over again, in the hope of reaping a little extra profit.

The commentary below is satisfactory for the average fashion show. It is about the right length and it covers the points usually stressed in a single garment. Naturally, the model is expected to display the various features of the coat at appropriate points.

Here is the very newest in smart fleece coats being worn this spring. Betty Simpson of Millard Fillmore Junior High School is the model. Betty is wearing one of the newest colors for spring—Crab Pink. Notice the new length on this coat. It is quite a bit shorter than last season's coats and notice also the interesting details about the cuff which add interest to the otherwise straight lines of the coat. This coat comes in a hundred per cent virgin wool fleece and is available in such cheerful new colors as Lemonade Yellow and Cactus Green. A special feature is the new zip-out metallic lining with satin finish which provides extra warmth when needed. You'll be able to wear this coat earlier than usual and far into next fall. A budget-pleasing price of only $49.50 is another one of the features of this beautiful new coat. Martin's—Third Floor.

Interviews

Seldom done, though productive of some excellent results, is the interviewing of people before a live audience. Such interviewing is done extensively on the radio or television, but the possibilities are equally good when the master of ceremonies entertains before an audience in person.

The interview has particular value at anniversary dinners or on occasions when historical highlights may be of special importance. Old-timers can be brought to the microphone and interviewed about their early days, or the early days of the organizations they represent.

People of this sort are often speakers of dubious quality, since they are inclined to ramble on indefinitely. The interview provides one way of keeping them under control. In addition, reluctant persons may be induced to appear, since all they are asked to do is answer questions, and no particular preparation is required of them.

When you are handling a program in this fashion, arrange to see your subjects several days in advance, or at least go over the material with them at the earliest possible opportunity. Make notes of the conversation and formulate your questions from these. The people with whom you are working may offer suggestions as to suitable topics for conversation or, if not, the interviewer can ask leading questions that may release a flow of valuable information for inclusion on the program later.

Organize the questions yourself, but indicate only in a general way to your subject the course of the questions to be asked. In that way, you keep the interview more spontaneous and retain control over its progress.

Later after you have carefully arranged an outline of your questions, the other half of the interview may appear with a second set as long as your arm. When this happens, it may prove embarrassing to avoid using some of them, but unless something of unusual interest turns up—and this is not likely to happen—stick to the original set of questions.

Neither is it advisable to go over the questions and answers again and again at a pre-presentation rehearsal. Try to keep everything as informal as possible. With the conditions under which you are working, it is highly unlikely that you are going to make any deathless contributions to the literature of the spoken word. Therefore, it is better to keep everything perfectly casual and try to have a little fun than it is to get yourself and your subject all tied up in knots.

Results are usually better if you restrict each interview to a single subject or to a single phase of a subject. In that way, you prevent the interview from wandering too far afield.

The following is a capsulized version of an interview similar to the one suggested earlier at a Pioneers' Banquet. Names, places and incidents are largely fictional, although the author has staged a similar interview under similar circumstances.

EMCEE: In our interview with some of the old-timers from this area, we cannot afford to neglect the city of Hillville. One of the pioneers there was Mrs. Herbert Fudnuk, wife of an early day miner. She has a story to tell about one of the pioneer industries of Hillville, one that I'm sure most of us never even knew existed. I'm going to bring Mrs. Fudnuk to our microphone and ask her a few questions about this circumstance.

MRS. FUDNUK: It wasn't an industry, really.

EMCEE: What was it then?

MRS. FUDNUK: You know. I told you earlier.

EMCEE: Yes, but I'd like to have you tell me again for the benefit of this audience. How old were you then?

MRS. FUDNUK: About ten or twelve.

EMCEE: How long ago was that?

MRS. FUDNUK: Oh, that would be telling. Let's just say it was before the turn of the century.

EMCEE: All right. We've got that established. Did you live in Hillville then?

MRS. FUDNUK: Oh, no. We lived in the country. On a farm about ten or twelve miles out of town.

EMCEE: You and your family?

MRS. FUDNUK: Yes.

EMCEE: How many were there?

MRS. FUDNUK: Besides myself, I had nine brothers and sisters.

EMCEE: And what did you raise beside children?

MRS. FUDNUK: Watermelons.

EMCEE: What's so amazing about that?

MRS. FUDNUK: Did you ever hear of watermelons being raised at Hillville?

EMCEE: No, I don't believe I ever did.

MRS. FUDNUK: And you never will again!

EMCEE: And why is that, Mrs. Fudnuk?

MRS. FUDNUK: Too cold. It's too high up in the mountains.

EMCEE: Well, tell me, how did it happen, this one particular time?

MRS. FUDNUK: My father had brought the watermelon seeds with him when he came from the east. That first summer at Hillville we thought we'd try to plant some of them. We did. They grew fine. We planted them again the next year and for several years after, but they never grew again. They never matured. We were never able to grow watermelons again as long as we tried.

EMCEE: Why was that, Mrs. Fudnuk?

MRS. FUDNUK: The frost came too early. That one year, we just happened to have a longer growing season. The frost held off until nearly the end of September. It never happened again.

EMCEE: Remarkable! But I told our audience here that this was an industry. How about it, Mrs. Fudnuk? Were you able to sell your watermelons that one year.

MRS. FUDNUK: Oh, yes. We took a wagon load into Hillville. The miners had never seen a watermelon—most of them—since they'd come into the country. They snapped them up for a dollar apiece. We made more money off the farm that summer than we did for almost twenty years.

EMCEE: I think that's wonderful! Thank you, Mrs. Fudnuk, for your excellent story. I think it's rather an interesting sidelight on history. In all its existence—and that's almost a hundred years—there's only one year in which home grown watermelons have been successfully sold in Hillville!

Specialty Bits

If you work very long as a master of ceremonies, you are certain, sooner or later, to appear in a sketch or blackout bit that may be presented as part of a larger entertainment. In fact, the practice is almost universal.

When sketches are of a dramatic nature, with costumes and the elements of scenery, there is usually a dramatic director who sees to it that the skits are properly staged.

There is, however, another matter which the master of ceremonies will have to decide for himself. Whenever he appears in a skit, he must make sure at the end that there is time for him to change back into his regular costume. He must be able to appear, calm and equable, prepared to make his next announcement and not look as though he had just run forty miles in order to make it.

As a practical matter, this means that if costumes are used, they must be of an elemental sort, such as robes, gowns, cloaks, and the like, worn over the regular clothes of the master of ceremonies and quickly discarded at the end.

There is another situation, though, where the average dramatic director will prove to be of only slight value. That is where the master of ceremonies appears as a straight man for a comedian.

A straight man is sometimes known as a stooge, but that definition is not entirely correct. Originally a stooge meant only a man who heckled a comedian from a seat located somewhere in the auditorium, usually a box. Later a stooge meant any one of a number of assistant comedians who worked as a group in heckling the principal comedian on the stage. Later still, the term "stooge" came to mean any person who worked with a comedian. But a stooge is not really a straight man. Stooges frequently get laughs of their own; a straight man rarely does. The straight man, as he positively will be known in this peroration and as he will be played by the average master of ceremonies, is a well-dressed person who asks questions of a comedian so that the latter can make with the funny answers.

That is all there is to it except that, as a straight man, unless you follow a number of very simple rules, your alleged comedy act will run itself into the ground. To prevent that eventuality from taking place, here are the points which must be kept in mind: (1) **Tempo.**—The straight man is primarily responsible for maintaining the tempo of the repartee. He should not be permitted to drag his feet but should start speaking promptly as soon as the laugh preceding begins to die. Then he should speak his line clearly and with despatch. (2) **Inflection.**—Always be careful to accent the word or phrase on which the laugh depends. In the classic example, "Who was that **lady** I seen you with last night?," accent the word "lady," because the laugh in the lines, "That wasn't no lady; that was my wife!", depends upon the recognition of the word "lady" in the first sentence. (3) Stillness.—The straight man moves no more than is absolutely necessary when speaking his own lines and moves not at all when listening to the comedian, which he does with rapt attention. (4) Reaction.— Though the straight man remains quiet while the comedian is speaking, after the punch line is delivered, his reaction should be immediate and violent. If not immediate, it should be violent—more violent than when immediate—because with the "slow take," it is essential to accent more heavily the fact that the point of the gag has finally arrived.

If this sounds like the formula for nuclear fission, watch some of the short one-reel comedies on the screen, and you will quickly discover what is meant by the "slow take."

You will then discover that the "slow take" applies to a situation in which one of the characters is unable to understand the full meaning of a joke until considerable time has elapsed. He then reacts all the harder. The "slow take" indicates that it has taken considerable time for the meaning of the joke to penetrate his thick skull. The audience is then left with the pleasant sensation of being considerably smarter than those dumbbells up there on the screen. As a result, they laugh all the harder.

For example, reverse the joke already outlined. The comedian asks the straight man, "Did you see that lady I was out with last night?" "No," answers the straight man. "Who was she?" The comedian then laughs and asserts, "That wasn't no lady. That was your wife!"

Instead of seeing the point of this brilliant bit immediately, the straight man continues the conversation. Then, all of a sudden, it dawns on him that the comedian said something different from what was expected. It is this sudden dawning, the delayed reaction which is known as the "slow take."

But to get back to the matter of what might be called the regular reaction: It is one of the most important parts of any comedy routine. As was noted earlier, it is really the reaction which gets the laugh. The entire success of the act depends upon it. The disgust, the surprise, the other emotions displayed by the straight man help to build the laughs originally created by the comedian.

The process can be outlined as a course of action which takes place around the three sides of a triangle. First, the eyes of the audience are on the straight man as he asks the question. Then they travel over to the comedian as he responds. Finally, as the comedian delivers his laugh-provoking clincher, the eyes of the audience shift back to the straight man to watch for his reaction. If his reaction comes at the psychological moment, at the instant the audience is prepared to laugh, all is well with the act. If not, there is certain to be a decrease in the number of laughs and in the volume of those which are received. It is through a variety of reactions, fast or slow, long or short, that a comedy act gains the vitality and change of pace it needs to survive the number of minutes it remains on the stage.

Of course, the comedian adds something to the act, too, and there must be basically funny material—jokes and repartee. But the information given here is from the viewpoint of the straight man, and the best comedy act in the world will not register with an audience unless the straight man does his part as well.

The contribution of the straight man is to phrase his question in such a manner that the point of the joke becomes obvious, and also to react to the comedian's funny reply in such a manner that the laughter of the audience is prolonged.

Unless you are something of a comedian yourself, you will find it much easier to work with one during those pauses where extensible stories were suggested. You will find it much easier than trying to fill the space all by yourself. If a brief two-man comedy routine can be inserted, the show will doubtless seem to move along much faster and the audience may never even guess that a stage wait has been in progress.

For best results, on the stage or anywhere else except the

radio, try to use gags which have visual appeal. Use jokes which call for a display of action, instead of those which are strictly conversational.

Inexperienced performers find it much easier to maintain the spirit and pace of jokes that must be told to the accompaniment of a certain amount of action.

The following dialogue might be quoted as an example.

Straight Man (As the **Comedian** enters wearing a funny hat). Where did you get that hat?

Comedian (Blankly blinking). What hat?

Straight Man. The one on your head, you dope!

Comedian. Oh, that! (Removes his hat, peers into it.) That's my magician's hat.

Straight Man (Scoffingly). Let's see you do a trick.

Comedian. O. K. (Reaches into his hat and pulls out something between his thumb and forefinger which is completely invisible.) There!

Straight Man. What's that?

Comedian. It's a rabbit.

Straight Man. Rabbit? I don't see any rabbit.

Comedian. Of course you don't! It's a hair! (He ducks as the **Straight Man** moves as if to strike him.)

The move of the straight man to strike the comedian is what is known as a violent reaction.

Minstrels

There are other ways in which the master of ceremonies can work an entertainer. One of these is in the minstrel. Here the master of ceremonies is known as the interlocutor. His duties are fairly prescribed. In the minstrel first-part, he acts as a straight man in the repartee with the endmen and announces the specialty bits as they occur. In the second part—the afterpiece or olio—he may appear in the sketches. But his work is usually confined to front-of-the-curtain announcements of the various numbers and to occasional appearances as straight man with a comedian.

Though pleasant, the interlocutor is usually very reserved and illustrates perfectly the thesis that a durable master of ceremonies, even in so broad an entertainment as a minstrel, is more closely identified with the audience than he is with the performers on the stage.

An Individual Specialty

Many times, if you appear quite often in vaudeville shows or revues, the question will arise, "Do you have a specialty of your own?" It is not essential for the amateur master of ceremonies to have a specialty. But if you are going to do a considerable amount of work for pay, the question will inevitably be asked.

A specialty is some single entertainment bit that you may be able to contribute to the program in addition to your announcing chores. It may be magic, or a vocal selection. The ability to sing is particularly useful during production numbers, when a line of chorus girls appear and it is necessary for someone to add a vocal solo to the music. Magic tricks are excellent for those long pauses for which extensible stories were suggested. There are any number of other ideas which the imaginative master of ceremonies can incorporate into his repertoire.

Hand puppets can be used, or even marionettes can be manipulated by strings in full view of the audience. Tap dancing is a suitable specialty for a master of ceremonies, although it has the disadvantage of leaving him out of breath when it comes time to introduce the next number.

In any case, the specialty chosen should not require many additional props or an elaborate change of costume. For instance, if magic is used, it should be possible to carry the equipment in the pocket.

There may be exceptions to this rule, but because of the nature of his work, it should be possible for the master of ceremonies to dispose of his equipment at the end of his performance with the greatest possible ease. He cannot be encumbered when he goes on to introduce the next act on the program. So for the best success choose only those specialties which require a minimum of easily handled equipment or none at all.

CHAPTER NINE

ON THE AIR

The subject of radio announcing can fill a book in itself, but there are a number of program types on which the non-professional can expect to appear from time to time. There are also programs, modeled after radio broadcasts, which are presented before a live audience without actually going on the air. These two types alone will be considered.

The Radio Announcer

When most people think of a radio announcer, they think of someone with a big deep voice and they think of little else. Though a good voice is vital, it is not the single most important element in radio work.

The most important factor is visualization, the ability to see, to feel the great invisible audience and to appeal to it directly. Strangely enough, this audience, despite its size, cannot be visualized en masse. It is necessary to visualize and to speak to the members of your audience as individuals.

Do not, therefore, adopt the frenzied tones of the orator seeking to move millions while you saw the air with grandiloquent gestures and wake the dead with a torrent of sound.

Radio is intimate. Though you may be addressing an audience numbering into the hundreds of thousands, you must keep your efforts scaled to the single individual who may be listening all by himself in a lonely room. Who is he—this listener in a distant living room? What are his interests? His tastes? The decision here is up to you. It is the accuracy of your judgment, based upon the material you are presenting, which will, in large measure, determine your success.

To illustrate: If you are presenting a newscast, you are giving information to people who are primarily interested in finding out what is going on in the world. It pays then to be concise and to present the news with a reasonable degree of understanding. No one cares whether you are a great dramatic artist, but you must be clear and logical in the presentation of your material. If, on the other hand, you are trying to sell a certain brand of soap, you will get much farther if you display, at least by inference, a ready sympathy with the problems of the harried housewife. You outline the superiority of your product and try to induce action—which is something different from the presentation of mere factual information.

These are only two examples, but they illustrate perfectly the point that is being made. The lady interested in soap may require information, but she also needs the sympathetic attention of someone who has an interest in her problem. If the newscaster were to employ the same unctuous approach, he would no longer be a newscaster but a propagandist.

Musical Programs

In reality, there are only two types of musical programs— one serious, the other light. There are varying shades of difference between them. You can also have light music on a serious program or vice versa, although the latter is very uncommon. The point is not made to confuse but to clarify a distinction that almost always is prevalent in the presentation of any kind of music.

On the surface, it would seem that music should be presented for simple enjoyment, but such is not always the case. There has grown up around the presentation of serious music such a quantity of ritual and cliché that, if you attempt to announce a program in simple English, you will be driven from the temple with whips. The result is that most announcers of serious music sound as though they were suffering from a severe case of adenoids. It is well, perhaps, that serious music be presented seriously, but it scarcely seems suitable that it always be presented in the hushed tones so commonly used.

It should be possible for you to do a good, simple, straightforward job of presenting serious music, but things being what they are, you will probably not succeed. You will have to compromise. You might like to say, "Richard Wagner" when you refer to the composer of the operas, using the accepted English pronunciation. On a serious program, however, you will probably have to intone nasally, "Reee-kard Vaahg-ner." You will produce a great effect, but you will also sound a trifle silly.

At the same time, you will discover to your dismay, that there is a considerable difference of opinion as to how the names of the various composers should be pronounced. The same confusion applies to musical terms. You either have to strike out blindly, or you learn the ritual patiently by trial and error.

Let it be said right at the outset that most good musicians do not care how you pronounce the words. It is not the performer who causes you to worry. He knows that the music will carry itself. It is the super-colossal musical intelligentsia, barely able to pick out "Chopsticks" on the piano, who cause you all the trouble, and they can be very troublesome indeed.

Whichever attitude you adopt, whether it be simple and unaffected or grandiose and dull, will be determined somewhat by the type of audience before which you are appearing. If it is composed of the musical cognoscenti, interested in maintaining good music as a closed corporation, you may have trouble. If not, you may be able to use a species of simple English.

The subject is important because the snobbishness with which much serious music is presented interferes with its penetration into groups that might, with profit, learn to appreciate it. Radio, for instance, did a good job of popularizing serious music for a number of years. Then serious music becomes increasingly difficult to find on the air because, among other things, its presentation had become so encrusted with ritual that there is little time left in which to play the tune. The tone of the presentation has been such that it repels the average listener. The holier-than-thou attitude has made him believe that serious music is too difficult to understand, and so he has ignored its performance and dialed to Spud McDudd and His Wildcats.

By this time, you are now asking, "What has this to do with me? How can I solve the problem?"

Well, you need not try to solve the entire difficulty yourself, but you can strike a blow for common sense. You can, when the opportunity presents itself, Anglicize a name or find a simpler method of introducing a piece of music. Then be content. If you are persistent, eventually the rest of the world may catch up with you, and you will thus gain the satisfaction of having done something genuinely useful.

However, there is one point which ought to be remembered. A serious piece of music will frequently need a sizable background fill-in in order to be properly appreciated. Something of the sort must be done, at least until such time as everyone has a wider or more varied knowledge of music. Until that happy day or until fashions change and audiences can enjoy serious music without the accompanying snobbery, it may be best to do a little research and announce that the Debussy "Quartet in G Minor" is the only work of its kind by the composer, that it received its debut in 1893 and that, despite an unfavorable reception at its first playing, it has since come to be recognized as a masterwork of its kind.

It is all a question of attitude. If you present these facts in such a way that they might conceivably add to the enjoyment of the audience, that is one thing. If you do it merely to parade your own knowledge, that is something else again. Needless to say, the last approach should not be encouraged.

With this discussion out of the way, it is now possible to get on to some of the more practical aspects of presenting musical programs before a live audience or on the radio.

First of all, you have to tell who is playing and indicate the general nature of the program. This need not be too difficult. The following announcement might serve as an example. "You are invited to hear the first concert of the season by the Podunk High School Orchestra. On the program today, we are to hear several overtures and a waltz by Straus. The orchestra, conducted by Wilbur Fudnuk, musical instructor at the school, begins with the overture to 'Orpheus in the Underworld' by Offenbach." If you are announcing the program before the high school assembly, it may not be necessary to stress the fact that the orchestra is conducted by Mr. Fudnuk. His name, however, should be inserted at the earliest opportunity, both as a compliment to the conductor and for the benefit of anyone who does not know who he is.

In a situation like this, you should ask yourself these questions, "Who or what is this musical group I am presenting? Who is the leader? How well will they be known to the audience? What kind of music will they be playing? If I were seated in the audience, what would I want to know about them before the concert started? What would I need to know to appreciate the music?" By asking these questions and by figuring out the answers, you perform your principal function as a master of ceremonies.

As fast as possible, get into the first number on the program. Nothing is quite so deadly as to delay the start of a musical program with a superfluity of talk. If there is information which must be given, weave it into the program wherever possible as you go along, but keep it short.

If you are on the air, during the course of the broadcast, you must occasionally remind your listeners as to who is playing. You might do this for the benefit of those late tuners-in who might be interested in knowing what is happening. On the air, also, you give a recapitulation at the end. You have heard the radio announcer do it a thousand times: "From the beautiful Terrace Room of the Hotel Plitz-Plotz-on-the-Hudson, etc." In this way, those who may have missed parts of it earlier can catch up with the proceedings before you leave the air. Each time you repeat the information, however, you should try to do it in a different way, to lend a greater variety to your performance.

In a live program, it is necessary to thank those present for their attention and, if the performers appeared for nothing, it is only courtesy to thank them profusely for the display of their talents.

As for those difficult musical names, there is no substitute for the use of a good musical dictionary. You will find most musical terms listed in the main section. Composers' names may be found in the biographical section. If you cannot find the information you require, ask some of your musical friends. When they cannot tell you—and this happens with surprising frequency—forget the whole thing or do the best you can, although there are books of musical commentary and popular record information at the public library which may be of some help. Under average conditions, however, you will find that there simply is not enough time to search out the more esoteric items. Who, for instance, knows what a branslés is without considerable research? When local facilities do not provide the answer, you may have to ignore the entire problem or skip around it the best you can. This statement may sound irresponsible, but as a practical matter it may prove to be the only solution.

On a program of popular music considerable more latitude is allowed. It is quite permissible to joke about the numbers, to make puns out of the titles, or to weave them into a story.

But you do have to be consistent throughout the entire program. For instance, it will not do to announce the major part of a program in a fairly straight-faced manner and then come out with an outrageous pun just because you happened to think of it. If you announce the first number in a comic vein, you are in duty bound to continue the rest of the program in the same vein. Besides, if you tell a good joke in the middle of a sober-sided program, it may creep on the audience without anyone's being aware of what has happened. If you tell the story and it fails to get a laugh, you might as well have saved your breath, anyway. Besides, way back in Chapter Two, some mention was made of coherence. This is a perfect example of what was meant.

However, a change of pace will do no harm. If you have been plodding along in a simple and straightforward manner, a mild attempt at humor may serve to salt the situation, provided you are announcing a number that seems to call for it. The question here is of taste. If you can vary the pattern—but not too much—you will get along much better than if you try to make all of your announcements in the same stiff and unyielding manner.

There are three things which ought to be remembered when formulating an announcement: the music, the performer, and the arrangement. The problem is to decide which is the most important or which requires the more concise treatment when presented to the audience.

Take as an example the aria, "My Heart at Thy Sweet Voice," from the opera, "Samson and Delilah." On this occasion, it will not be sung as in the opera but will be played in special arrangement by a dance band, and as a specialty one of the members of the orchestra will give a whistling solo. Now it will not do to present this melody as though it were only another popular tune. It must be announced as an arrangement, or anyone who knows better will get very irritated with you. Then since the band is apparently using the arrangement as a specialty and featuring the whistling soloist, he must figure prominently in the introduction.

Your announcement of the number may be something like the following: "Deacon Bones and His Back-Room Boys now play a special arrangement of 'My Heart at Thy Sweet Voice' from the opera, 'Samson and Delilah.' As an added attraction, we're going to hear the Deacon himself whistle a chorus or two, just to show you that it can be done."

Thus when you cover all the essential points, the audience does not have to guess. They know what's going on. They can lean back and enjoy themselves.

Incidentally, when presenting an arrangement of some old familiar tune or classic melody, do not handle it as though it were yesterday's production from some submerged genius in Tin Pan Alley. Those who know better will not like you very well.

Try to indicate, too, those tunes which come from the

Broadway stage or the motion pictures. By inserting this information in your announcements, you not only add to your customers' enjoyment but you help to keep them abreast of the latest developments in the field. If you get the chance, examine the music before you make the announcement. The information you require about composers, source, etc., can be found somewhere on the copy, if you look hard enough.

In general, the accent should be on the music or the performer and not on the announcer. Unless you are especially adept at the job, keep the introductions on a musical program as short as possible.

If you were to examine the script of the average program on the radio, you would be amazed at how short they really are. The musicians have to work like mad in order to keep up with the pace of the program.

Here are three examples of typical musical programs. The first is for a program of popular music.

ANNOUNCER *(Cold.)** It's Rippling Rhythm Time!

BIZ *(Begin Rippling effect.)*

ANNOUNCER *(Over effect.)* Conrad Corntassel plays!

MUSIC *(Corntassel theme.)*

ANNOUNCER. It's the Rippling Rhythms of Conrad Contassel and His Orchestra, speeding your way tonight from the beautiful Penthouse Roof atop the Hotel Villa Grande in downtown Tuba City. While Tuba City dances to the music of Conrad Corntassel and His Orchestra, join us while the maestro opens his program with today's top tune—Dogpatch Serenade.

MUSIC *(Dogpatch Serenade.)*

ANNOUNCER. Rippling Rhythms are enhanced now by the lovely voice of Dolores Smith, as she joins the orchestra to sing a song of romantic anticipation—Tonight's the Night.

MUSIC *(Tonight's the Night.)*

ANNOUNCER. Conrad Corntassel dons serape and nine-gallon sombrero to take us south of the border for the Latin-American favorite—Mucho, Mucho.

MUSIC *(Mucho, Mucho.)*

ANNOUNCER. It's the music of Conrad Corntassle and His Rippling

---

* "Cold" means beginning the program without a musical fanfare or introductory musical theme.

Rhythms reaching you from the Penthouse Roof of the Hotel Villa
Grande in Tuba City. Again it's Delores Smith who returns to our
microphone and joins the orchestra in another romantic hit from the
day's top favorites—I'm Enchanted.

MUSIC *(I'm Enchanted.)*

ANNOUNCER. There's a clear track ahead as the trio joins Conrad
Corntassel and His Orchestra for a fast moving version of—The Locotown Express.

MUSIC *(Locotown Express.)*

BIZ *(Segue ** to theme.)*

ANNOUNCER *(Over theme.)* From the beautiful Penthouse Roof of
the Hotel Villa Grande in Tuba City, we have presented the unique
Rippling Rhythms of Conrad Corntassel and His Orchestra. Vocals were
by Delores Smith and the trio. Join us again when next we bring you—
the Rippling Rhythms of Conrad Corntassel and His Orchestra.

BIZ *(Rippling effect, then cut back to theme till time.)*

ANNOUNCER. This is the Continental Broadcasting System!

The broadcast of a high school orchestra concert provides
the mythical situation with which we are next to be concerned.

ANNOUNCER. Good evening! From the stage of the Tuba City Community High School, we present the annual concert of the high school
orchestra under the direction of John Jefferson Monroe. Forty-five strong,
these young musicians have been rehearsing since last September for
what, over the years, has grown to be one of the outstanding musical
events in the life of Tuba City. Before an audience of parents and friends,
the program opens with the overture to the "Festival of Eros" by Faellen-
bach.

MUSIC *(Overture—Festival of Eros.)*

ANNOUNCER. A descriptive waltz is next—*Springtime Flowers* by the
Swedish-American composer—Axel Peterkin. The composer's notes for
this captivating musical tidbit read as follows: "In my mind's eye, I see
a field covered with blue and yellow flowers. The breeze blows. The
flowers sway in the breeze until, in the mind of the beholder, they all
join in the rhythms of the waltz." Springtime Flowers by Axel Peterkin.

MUSIC *(Springtime Flowers.)*

ANNOUNCER. From the stage of the high school auditorium we are
presenting the annual concert of the Tuba City Community High School
orchestra under the direction of John Jefferson Monroe. We hear next
a novelty march—Entry of the Teddy Bears by Theodore Gluck.

MUSIC *(Entry of the Teddy Bears.)*

ANNOUNCER. Marjorie Mayer is soloist in this next number we are

---

** Means to join two pieces of music together without pause.

to hear played by the Tuba City Community High School Orchestra. Miss Mayer, a fifteen year old Junior, will play the trumpet against a background of folk melodies entitled—Italian Potpourri.

Music *(Italian Potpourri.)*

Announcer. Conductor Monroe now leads his young musicians through a program piece about life in America at the turn of the century. Entitled "Prelude to the Fourth of July," we hear first the gentle sounds of the morning breeze heralding the approach of another warm day. Then comes the early burst of distant firecrackers. The celebration reaches its climax in the parade at noon when the town band marches briskly down the street to the full-throated sound of trumpets and trombones. Here is "Prelude to the Fourth of July" by Faustus Goldbeat.

Music *(Prelude to the Fourth of July.)*

Announcer. The martial beat continues as the orchestra, under John Jefferson Monroe, plays the Swczy march—Hammer and Tongs.

Music *(Hammer and Tongs.)*

Announcer. This has been the annual concert of the Tuba City High School Orchestra, presented from the stage of the high school auditorium under the direction of John Jefferson Monroe. Marjorie Mayer was trumpet soloist. Our thanks to each of the participating musicians. And from them to you, greetings from the entire student body of Tuba City Community High School. This is Barton Barton speaking.

Biz *(Reprise Hammer and Tongs till time.)*

* * * *

A still more serious program might be the following:

Announcer. Good afternoon. We are speaking from the sanctuary of the Tuba City Community Church where this afternoon we are privileged in hearing a brief radio concert on the new Mower organ which has just been installed in the church. The concert will be played by Mr. Fritz Wurfel, organist at the City Church in Plainfield and instructor in the Plainfield Conservatory of Music. The new organ in the Tuba City Community Church is the result of a campaign begun last January by the members of the congregation when more than forty thousand dollars were subscribed for the purchase of the instrument you are about to hear. This radio concert is in the nature of a preview for the public service of dedication which will be held in the church this evening beginning at eight o'clock and to which the public is cordially invited. Our concert this afternoon begins with the Toccata and Fugue in D Minor by Barbizon.

Music *(Toccata and Fugue.)*

Announcer. Mr. Wurfel will now play one of his own compositions —Melody in G. Although this is the first time that Mr. Wurfel's composition has been played on the air, it has been heard on several previous occasions when it was well received because of its sprightly yet sober air of meditation.

Music *(Melody in G.)*

ANNOUNCER. You have heard *Melody in G* by Fritz Wurfel played by the composer himself on the new Mower organ only recently installed in the Tuba City Community Church. Several familiar themes from Bach are now combined in a composition requiring the utmost in technical dexterity by the performing artist. Mr. Wurfel now plays the Grand Fantasia for Organ in F Major arranged by Zinsmer.

Music *(Grand Fantasia.)*

ANNOUNCER. For the past quarter hour, we have presented a radio preview of the public dedicatory concert being played this evening by Mr. Fritz Wurfel of Plainfield on the new Mower organ which has just been installed in the Tuba City Community Church. The listening public is cordially invited to attend this concert which begins tonight at eight o'clock in the church sanctuary. Mr. Wurfel is organist at the City Church in Plainfield and instructor in Organ Theory at the Plainfield Conservatory of Music. This is Duncan Duncan speaking and returning you to our main studios.

* * * *

Lest these scripts seem repetitious, remember that they are only the skeleton, the outline as it were, of the entire program. Several minutes of music may elapse between each announcement, minutes during which a score or more or even hundreds of listeners may tune in or out. It is essential, therefore, that you repeat at intervals the basic information which is required for a proper enjoyment of the program.

Round-Table Discussions

If you read the newspapers regularly, subscribe to a half dozen leading periodicals, and listen to all of the important commentators on the radio, you might be able to do a halfway decent job of acting as moderator on a round-table discussion. To qualify for this position, you will find it very important to keep abreast of the news and to have a broad understanding of major political and economic trends.

However, since shortcomings in this respect have not deterred others, there is probably no reason why you should not go ahead and try your hand without all of the necessary qualifications. You will doubtless be able to do quite as well as some of the others who have made the attempt.

You will have to make a special effort to ground yourself in the elements of the subject under discussion. You will have to achieve this through either reading or by questioning those who are qualified to give you the necessary information. Sometimes your best sources will be those who are to appear on the program itself.

Despite a widely held illusion to the contrary, it is not essential to arrive at any conclusion on a round-table discussion. The principal purpose of such a discussion is to present a variety of viewpoints so that the auditor can make up his own mind or, at least, can give the subject a little thought. Of course, there is no reason why a round-table discussion cannot lead to a conclusion, but this is scarcely to be expected. As a matter of fact, with really good people on your program—expert partisans who are able to maintain a good argument—it should prove quite impossible to force a conclusion. They will hold to their own points of view too tenaciously. Who, for instance, could ask a public power proponent to change his point of view in the brief time allotted for a round-table discussion? You may achieve agreement on minor issues, but hardly more than that is to be expected.

A favorite trick in certain groups is to present a so-called round-table discussion, with everyone talking and arguing on the same side, as though there were no opposition to the subject being presented. Such a performance is only a subterfuge, if not a deliberate attempt to mislead and is, in no sense, a round-table discussion. There must be disagreement if there is to be an effective presentation of the issues.

Your biggest job, when preparing a discussion, is to assemble a group of competent people with divergent opinions and the courage and stamina to present them. You may have to do this work yourself, it may be done for you by a special committee, or if the program is being broadcast or televised, it may be done by the program personnel of the station.

In any case, try to brief yourself on the backgrounds of

those who are to appear with you on the discussion. Not only will you be able to start the discussion more intelligently, but it breeds a greater feeling of confidence in those participants who may be meeting you for the first time. They are deeply concerned and if you show a ready sympathy for their trials and tribulations plus a certain knowledge of the problems facing them, they are going to have considerably more confidence in your ability to handle the program.

The search for people with divergent opinions does not mean that you must seek only those who have diametrically opposed viewpoints about the subject under discussion. In the first place, you will rarely find two people in complete disagreement on any subject broad enough to make a good round-table discussion. If there are certain areas of agreement, it is desirable to narrow the arguments down to those few points on which there is a dispute.

As much as possible, the participants on your program should be recognized authorities, or they should represent organizations known to have a responsible interest in the subject under consideration. For instance, in a discussion on a school bond issue, one representative might be from the Parent-Teachers' Associations, the other from the Taxpayers' League.

Care should be taken to see that the contestants are evenly matched in other qualities as well, such as their speaking ability. It does not pay to load the dice in a round-table discussion. If there is any appearance of unfairness, the weaker side automatically gains the sympathy of the audience and the effectiveness of the arguments is vitiated. Every effort should be made to keep the discussion scrupulously fair. If the participants are unwilling to appear on that basis, the subject should be dropped immediately or another set of participants procured.

If the moderator is to serve his most useful purpose, he must summarize the conflicting viewpoints at the end. For this, if for no other reason, he must have some understanding of what is taking place in the course of the discussion.

How much rehearsal to have beforehand is a vexing question. Some people like to work from a fairly elaborate outline. Others prefer simply to pick a starting point and let the discussion lead them where it will. Under most conditions, a policy somewhere between the two seems to work the best.

At the outset, there should be general agreement as to what the subject means. Lest this sound facetious, remember that many proponents of an idea can come up with the weirdest conceptions of what that idea is all about. Especially is this so if they have an ax to grind. For example, there was the butcher who showed up at Thanksgiving time prepared to do battle for the royal bird in a discussion entitled, "What Shall We Do About Turkey?"

Normally there should also be agreement on what the subject is not about. Or, to put it another way, there should be agreement on where the disagreement lies. This is far more important than discovering what precisely should be said during the course of a discussion. Ideas are important. The words and sentences are only the tools that express those ideas.

In every other detail, the discussion should be permitted to take its own course, with the moderator drawing the participants back into the fold, when they seem inclined to wander too far afield.

Before the start, each speaker should have in mind the main outlines of the arguments to be used by the other side. Each will be better able to formulate his own arguments in rebuttal as a result, and a neater, more concise job will result.

During the course of the pre-broadcast discussion—if it is being broadcast—the moderator should likewise make notes of the principal points to be covered. In that way he can keep abreast of developments as they occur and insert a fruitful question now and then, if need be. He should also take care that the discussion leads to some logical end where a summary can be presented.

A summary is not the same as a conclusion. A conclusion pre-supposes that the contestants have reached some agreement about the subject. A summary merely re-states the principal sources of disagreement in concise style.

Needless to say, although the moderator can direct the course of the discussion, he cannot exert any influence upon the type and content of any argument offered. That is beyond his prerogative. From time to time he may have the feeling that he is in duty bound to rescue a speaker from the results of his own folly, but that task lies in the mind of the listener, the public. The moderator's job is to bring those arguments out in the open where this final court of appeal can render a decision.

The moderator also makes sure that each side has approximately an equal amount of time in which to present its arguments. This arrangement means that neither side should be permitted to monopolize the discussion for any great length of time and that, if one side asks a question or states a case, the other should be given an equal opportunity to reply. There is no need to hold a stop watch on the proceedings, but an obvious fairness is necessary.

Other important duties likewise fall to the moderator. He must act the part of a quasi-listener. That is, he must be prepared to ask the question that might occur to the average listener and inject it into the course of the discussion at his earliest opportunity.

To ask these questions as the program moves along and to do it gracefully requires a high degree of visualization. You must imagine yourself in the place of the average listener and ask the question that he might ask, if he had the chance. Before small groups, this is not so difficult, but before a large general audience, when you are appearing on radio or television, you must try to ask those questions which would help the uninformed without sounding peurile to those who might know something about the subject.

Many times, too, the moderator will hear a technical term that might require further explanation. When he does, he should ask for that explanation at the earliest convenient moment without, of course, interrupting the flow of the arguments. Say simply, "A moment ago you used such-and-such a term. Would you mind explaining what it means?"

Whether you make the opening and closing announcements for the round-table depends on circumstances but, generally speaking, it is safer if someone else does the job for you. This announcer makes it unnecessary for you to switch from a formal introduction into an informal discussion, a transition which sounds awkward under the best of conditions. Someone else should announce the subject under discussion, the names of the participants and their qualifications and this should include yourself. You can then start with a broad outline of the points to be covered and a definition of terms.

At any rate, regardless of who makes the introductions, you will have to see to it that the qualifications of the people participating are properly emphasized, if it has not been done before. This point has been made previously, but it is neglected enough in practice to bear repeating. If the chairman who makes the introduction fails to say that one of your representatives is the president of the East Podunk Firemen's Protective Foundation, when that fact is essential to a full understanding of the subject, it will be necessary for you to weave this information into the fabric of your round-table discussion at some appropriate moment.

Lest this seem like belaboring the point, remember that such identification makes the speaker more responsible for what he says, and the public has the right to know. If he represents a particular viewpoint, the public has the right to know what that viewpoint is. If your participants are merely acting parts, in an effort to present information, the problem is not nearly so important. Even then, however, it clarifies things if the viewpoint of each person is clearly stated at the start of the program.

These things are some of the safeguards that you must exercise in the interests of free speech. If you give audiences anything less, you are not doing your full duty either to yourself or to those who are listening.

Basically, what you have in any round-table discussion is

an opening in which the subject is stated, the speakers introduced and qualified, and the subject defined, if need be. After that, two or three phases of the subject are developed, especially those parts in which disagreement exists. A summary is made, after which there may be an opportunity for questions. Then comes the closing.

What has been discussed thus far is the round-table at which controversial subjects are handled and a direct dispute is possible. There is another kind of round table—what might be called the expository type—where two or three qualified participants develop a single idea through the medium of questions put to them by the moderator or by one another. A typical example of this kind of discussion might be embodied in a round table on the subject of "What Are Today's Commercial Possibilities in Alaska?" with the theme developed by a shipper, a banker, and a resident of the territory.

Strictly speaking, such a discussion might more properly be called a panel. Round table is a generic term meaning a discussion conducted in a more or less informal manner. From a purely technical speech standpoint, the term means a group discussion in which those participating are not necessarily experts. When experts appear, the correct term is "panel discussion." When the experts discuss their viewpoints in a more formal manner, when each in turn gives a short statement, and when a short summary is presented at the end by the moderator or master of ceremonies, you have a symposium, although the term is not often used.

After any discussion, there may be an opportunity for questions, provided that you are appearing before a live audience. Here the moderator must use special caution to see to it that everyone has an equal chance to be heard. At the start, restrict the questions one to a person. Then after everyone has had a chance, it may be possible to go back and acknowledge the request of some exceptionally eager individual, but no one should be allowed to monopolize the question period.

Be very firm about this. Say calmly and decisively, "I am

sorry, but questions will be restricted one to a person, until all have had an opportunity to be heard." Someone may be offended, but it is the lesser of two evils to offend only a single person than to lose the goodwill of your entire audience.

The besetting sin of all question-and-answer periods is that they are permitted to run for too long a time. Questions should be short, snappy, and to the point. If they are not, the moderator should interrupt. Answers likewise should be germane. If the speaker shows a tendency to wander, bring him back to the subject. It can be done by reminding the speaker that time is short and by restating the original question.

When the question period is over, if someone has a query which he still thinks is important, he can discuss it with the speaker privately and not waste the time of the entire group. At the first sign of lagging, rap the gavel and bring the discussion to an end.

Occasionally you will find on your round table people who, because of the intensity of their opinions, wish to take up all the time and monopolize the meeting. They start talking and never stop. As the dispenser of justice in such a situation, you have no choice but to silence the offender. Say, "Mr. Jughead (substitute his name), I insist the other side have a chance to be heard. You have now talked for five minutes. If you do not end your arguments in a reasonable length of time, I am going to ask that you leave the hall (or the studio) until such time as the other side has a chance to be heard."

After such treatment, your recalcitrant friend may realize that he is out of order and attempt to preserve some sort of decorum. If not, you will have to see that he is ejected, or the proponents of the other side will hate you for life.

Verbal discussions have ended in fisticuffs. If that happens to you, all you can do is sit quietly on the sidelines and hope that the opponents knock each other out. It will do you no good to join in the fray.

Here is a shortened example of how a typical round-table discussion might be staged.

CHAIRMAN. "Should City Park be Turned into a Downtown Parking Area?" This question has been discussed pro and con for some time. Finally, sufficient signatures have been obtained on a petition to have the question placed on the ballot in the city election next January 4. To inform the club about this question we have invited two persons to appear in an informal discussion of the subject. They are Mrs. Todhunter Hall, president of the Women's Garden and Study Club, and Mr. Wendell Howley, chairman of the Piedmont Junction Traffic Commission. Moderator for this evening's discussion will be Mr. Glenn Berries, instructor in speech at the Piedmont Junction High School. Mr. Berries:

BERRIES. As with most discussions that are very close to our hearts, those which have been carried on this far about the parking situation in Piedmont Junction have been distinguished more by heat than by light. However, tonight, I think we can rectify that situation somewhat because we have two very able representatives of the opposing viewpoints present. Mr. Howley, to start with you, why has the city traffic commission found it necessary to recommend that City Park be turned into a parking area?

HOWLEY. Well, Mr. Berries, as you know, the parking situation in Piedmont Junction has been getting steadily worse for some time. It is practically impossible to come downtown now and find a place to leave your car. Parking meters have helped, but they haven't proved to be the entire answer. The traffic commission realizes that private parking lots or parking garages are the only solution, but they haven't been forthcoming. Meanwhile, the parking situation gets worse and worse. That is why we have recommended that City Park be turned into a parking lot. It would accommodate close to five hundred cars and would eliminate, we think, much of the congestion in the downtown area.

BERRIES. Mrs. Hall, you have heard a statement of at least a part of the case for this suggested change. What is your viewpoint in this matter?

HALL. I can agree with Mr. Howley that there is need for a change. Something must be done about our downtown parking situation, but I think the solution he proposes will only go to make it worse. In the first place, traffic surveys show that there are, at least, two thousand cars trying to get into the downtown section each day for which there is no room. We can't see where a parking lot for five hundred cars is going to help very much. Besides, Mr. Howley admits himself that destroying the natural beauty of City Park is no real solution. Additional lots will have to be built. Why have the city going into the car parking business? Why not leave that to private enterprise and the owners of private garages and parking lots?

HOWLEY. First of all, Mrs. Hall, I would like to answer one implication that you made in reference to this proposed parking area. We don't propose to destroy the natural beauty of City Park. We want to leave the trees. What we plan to do is surface the area, install parking meters and retain the park much as it is in its present state.

HALL. Mr. Howley, do you mean to tell me that you can get five hundred cars into City Park if you leave all the trees? Would you want to park there if there's a tree every twenty-five yards in each direction? How are you going to get five hundred cars on the lot under those conditions? It seems to me to be manifestly impossible.

HOWLEY. It would be necessary to chop down some of the trees in the middle of the park. That much we admit, but it wouldn't be necessary to chop down very many.

HALL. How many?

HOWLEY. We don't know. That would have to be decided after present plans have progressed.

BERRIES. Mr. Howley, hasn't it been planned to build flower bed borders and other bits of beauty if City Park is turned into a parking area?

HOWLEY. That's right. It's possible that City Park might look even more beautiful than it does now.

HALL. What you don't seem to realize is that some of those trees in City Park have been planted for more than fifty years. Our club was responsible for planting some of them. Now, you propose to chop them down. I don't see how you can possibly say that the park will continue to look as pretty as it does now.

BERRIES. Mrs. Hall, what about the lack of parking facilities downtown? Does your club have any solution?

HALL. We have the same solution that Mr. Howley has, private garages and parking lots. We don't see any merit in tearing down something it has taken fifty years to build merely to provide space for a few cars when it doesn't really solve the problem.

HOWLEY. What are we going to do, Mrs. Hall, when no one seems to want to build parking lots or garages?

HALL. There are a lot of old shacks in this town, business buildings that are an eyesore. Why can't they be torn down and turned into lots?

HOWLEY. The point is—they haven't been. In the meantime, the situation is getting worse. It's practically impossible now to come downtown and find a place to park while you shop. The downtown area is being ruined. Business is moving out. Property values may be depreciated. The situation is serious.

HALL. Why don't businessmen band together to build garages?

BERRIES. Has that been thought of, Mr. Howley?

HOWLEY. Yes, it has. Steps have been taken, but these things take a long time. They can't be accomplished overnight.

HALL. It also took a long time to grow those trees, Mr. Howley.

BERRIES. How about financing this job? As I understand the subject

—and correct me if I'm wrong—the city proposes to make the necessary changes in City Park. Is that right?

HOWLEY. Yes, it is.

HALL. That's another thing. Why should the rest of us be taxed when only a few of the downtown merchants are going to benefit?

HOWLEY. City Park could probably be turned into a paying proposition, Mrs. Hall. With the parking meters there, City Park would probably make money. It could be turned into a self liquidating project.

HALL. Then, why not do it on a private basis with private capital?

HOWLEY. That is the eventual plan, Mrs. Hall, but we've got to get started. The situation is serious.

BERRIES. What about this objection, Mr. Howley, that City Park is too far away from the center of town to be of much value as a parking lot?

HOWLEY. That we've got to realize, Mr. Berries. Piedmont Junction is no longer a prairie village. We've got to realize that we can no longer get right out of our automobiles and go into our places of business. These are some of the penalties of growth. We see, too, that some steps will have to be taken soon if the situation is not to become worse. That is why we recommend that City Park immediately be turned into a parking area. Later, perhaps, when the situation improves—if it does— it can be reconverted into a park.

HALL. We maintain that a spot of beauty shouldn't be destroyed as a temporary expedient. City Park has taken a long time to build. Its growth, too, has been a part of our city's growth. It is located in a spot where visitors to our city get a very good impression as they get off trains or busses. We feel that parking problems, if it is a business matter, should be left to business people and that the answer be found in a business-like way, through private parking lots and garages.

BERRIES. I think you both have stated your cases rather well. I think you both agree that there is some solution needed to the congested parking conditions in downtown Piedmont Junction. I think you both agree that there is only one real final solution, private lots and garages operated for profit. The crux of the situation seems to be that Mr. Howley recommends that City Park be turned into a parking area as an immediate solution to a very pressing problem while Mrs. Hall submits that long term losses would outweigh any temporary advantages that might result. Thank you both for being with us on our discussion this evening.

CHAIRMAN. You have heard a discussion on the subject "Should City Park be Turned into a Downtown Parking Area?" Participants in the discussion were Mr. Wendell Howley, chairman of the Piedmont Junction Traffic Commission, and Mrs. Todhunter Hall, president of the Women's Study and Garden Club. Your moderator was Mr. Glenn Berries, instructor in speech at the Piedmont Junction High School.

Interviews

When interviewing a person about his life, his experiences, or his opinions, place yourself in the position of those who are listening. Try not only to bring out those points which the listener might want to know if he had the opportunity to ask the questions himself, but in the more serious type of interview try to bring out those things which he ought to know. In an interview about China, for instance, ask those questions which will enable the listener to arrive at a better-informed opinion about the subject.

Remember that the listeners do not want to hear about you. When the person being interviewed answers a question, the temptation to insert a comment showing that you, too, know something about the subject is at times irresistible. But stifle that impulse to add an extra word or two. Your comments rarely add anything to the quality of an interview and serve only to take the spotlight from where it belongs—on the person being interviewed.

There is a place, however, where you can legitimately insert comment. That is where it is necessary to make a transition from one question to another. Frequently the person with whom you are talking will not make an answer that leads directly into the next question, or you may wish to refer to an answer previously given in order to make your next question seem more intelligent. When that happens, set up a background for the next question, so the listener understands why it is being asked. Here is an example: "Mr. Fudnuk, we understand there is a steadily developing feeling of animosity on the part of the Neutralanians toward America. In view of the past friendship between our country and the Neutralanians, it seems a bit strange. Why has this situation come about?"

When rehearsing an interview with a single person, it is well to go over the questions a little more thoroughly than is commonly done in the round-table discussion, although here, as elsewhere, circumstances alter cases. If you are working from a script, rehearse until you and the person being interviewed sound as though you were both speaking extemporaneously. To gain this effect, it is better to keep the interview on an informal basis and to spend most of the time for preparation on the development of ideas rather than on the exact wording.

If you do spend more time on the wording, you may find yourself faced with a horrible dilemma. If you are dealing with any but the most thoroughly trained and experienced speakers, during the course of the interview you may find the person interviewed trying to recall what was said at the rehearsal rather than following the flow of ideas. When that happens, questions will be thrown out of context, and any outline you may have prepared will probably have to be tossed out the window, because the speaker may remember one set of words that was used in answer to another question and vice versa. It all becomes a jumbled mess.

Rehearse enough so that you know what you are going to talk about and in what order you will present your ideas. You may leave the exact wording until the final rendition unless something must be quoted verbatim, in which case your speaker can read it. Remember, however, that you are in charge of the interview and, if the speaker tends to wander off into uncharted fields, bring him back promptly to the subject agreed upon beforehand.

All of which brings up another problem. When conducting interviews, you will occasionally run into people who think that, because you know nothing about the subject yourself, you are incapable of performing your duties. This is a little removed from the truth. It is your job to conduct the interview, his to know the subject thoroughly. Ask intelligent questions, and you will have no trouble. As a matter of fact, it may even be better if you do not know too much about the subject. In that case you will be better able to adapt yourself to the viewpoint of the average listener, who also may be presumed to know very little about it. However, it does not do to carry that assumption too far. The subject may be more generally known than you think. Therefore do not begin with material that is too elementary or that reaches too far back into the past. Give your audience credit for a little intelligence.

When interviewing someone, either in person or on the air, as a convenience and a courtesy both to the audience and to the speaker, use a simple warm-up question at the start. In so doing, you give the speaker a moment or two to get his bearings and the audience gets a chance to become accustomed to the sound of his voice. Do not, however, ask such an innocuous question that all your subject can do is answer "Yes" or No."

If your speaker is new to the area, give him a start by asking his personal impression of the town or section of the country in which he finds himself. While not strikingly original, the gambit, at least, has the virtue of allowing the speaker to ingratiate himself with his audience by making a few complimentary remarks. Never ask such a question, though, without warning your speaker beforehand that you are going to do it. If he has to hesitate before answering or gives the name of the wrong town, both of you may look a trifle silly.

No more than a lawyer with a witness are you permitted to lead the speaker, that is ask questions in such a way that the answer is already implied in the question itself. Here is an example: "You told me, Mr. Fudnuk, that the people of Holland are giving up wooden shoes in favor of leather. I presume that is because leather is becoming more available and cheaper. Is that right?" All that Mr. Fudnuk can do in such a situation is murmur a confused "Yes." The question should be re-worded as follows: "You told me, Mr. Fudnuk, that the people of Holland are giving up wooden shoes in favor of leather. Why is that?"

To be quite blunt about it, no one cares whether you know the answer to the question or not. The important thing is to find out what Mr. Fudnuk, who has been there and who has studied the subject, thinks or knows about it. That is the purpose of the interview. Such a course may be debilitating to your ego, but it is the only means by which you can possibly succeed.

Naturally, on every interview, the subject matter should be so organized that one phase leads directly into another. If you are talking about Holland, it will not do, for instance, to talk about the scarcity of wooden shoes and then switch over to the tulip crop before finally coming back to pick up a bit of unfinished business about the shoes. Exhaust what is going to be said about one subject before going on to another.

When you get through, there may be a summary at the end, but that is strictly up to you. Some subjects do not require a summary. One can be eliminated if it appears that there is insufficient time or that the subject is not weighty enough to need one.

The Amateur Show

The amateur show has been heard often enough on the radio. It is frequently seen on television. It is a type of program often employed by clubs or lodges when they are seeking something a trifle different in the way of entertainment. Therefore it behooves you to know something about it.

The successful presentation of an amateur show requires knowledge of many of the techniques which have been discussed previously. If you remember a few of the things that were said about stage deportment, you should have no trouble getting around the stage or playing area and seeing to it that your amateurs get the proper amount of applause. If you recall what was said about interviewing, you can bring out the salient points of the tyro's career in such a way that it might prove interesting to the audience. Finally, if you remember the points that were made about discovering the most salable features in any performance and dwelling on them, you are properly prepared for presenting the new act.

If you question the actors beforehand in front of the audience, remember that you are not only trying to acquaint the audience with the act but are also attempting to put the actors at ease and get the act off to a good start. Your questions should be worded in such a way that this purpose is accomplished. Do not try to make a hero of yourself by ridiculing an act or any part of its performance. Leave that to the audience. Some of them may not think you are very funny.

CHAPTER TEN

THE BANQUET TOASTMASTER

Throughout this volume, hints and suggestions of various kinds have been made which should be of help to you when serving as master of ceremonies or toastmaster at a banquet, luncheon, or dinner. Since, however, you will probably appear more at this type of function than at any other, a few additional suggestions might be in order.

Typical Jobs

What are some of the places where you will be asked to appear? Well, they are many. Church dinners, dedicatory and anniversary banquets, kick-off breakfasts for drives, the annual banquets of trade associations or organizations—these affairs are grist for your mill.

Nine times out of ten, the group before which you are appearing will have another interest besides partaking of food. That being true, it pays to offer some recognition of these special interests or, at least to show a sympathetic approach toward some of the problems that those in your audience are facing. If you are working before a group of farmers, know something about the state of the crops or the livestock market and work in an oblique reference whenever possible. If you are talking to druggists, think up a new twist to the yarn about the man who woke up the druggist in the middle of the night to buy a stamp. Not only will your audience warm up to you more rapidly if you show this lively interest in their affairs, but any sallies you make will be greeted with more laughter if they have a familiar ring.

Many times references to the special interests of your audience may sound like flattery. In a sense they are, but there is certainly no harm in showing a little genuine appreciation of the problems of those before whom you are speaking, and it may do some good.

It might be well to remember some of the rules which are given in textbooks on public speaking concerning the appeal to personal experience. If you can relate what you are saying to the personal experience of your auditors, you will get much further and they will enjoy it more than if you only engage in vague generalities about nothing in particular.

Sources

You are now asking yourself, "Where do I get such information? Must I read a whole book on stock raising in order to talk intelligently before a group of cattlemen? Must I do all this in order to introduce a singer or a couple of acrobats?"

No, practically speaking, you could probably get along without all this elaborate preparation. But you would do a much better job if you read the book or glanced through a trade magazine relating to the business in hand. However, since there is seldom time for such thoroughness, you adopt the next best procedure.

Try to find someone in the organization and talk to him before the meeting begins. Find out what is agitating the minds of your audience, whether it be tariffs, taxes, government controls, or the price of meat. In the case of a church, talk to the minister, the church secretary, or one of the older members. They can often give you hints about the personal aspects of life in the church which can prove invaluable. If it is some other function, find such a well and pump it dry. You will be surprised what you can do with a little information judiciously acquired in this fashion.

In dealing with trade association, you will generally find that your best source of information is the paid secretary—the man who actually runs the organization between the meetings of the officers and the board of directors. These people are paid to be articulate. They usually understand the larger aspects of any situation, whereas some of the others in the organization may only stutter or stammer around if you ask them a direct question. Try, if possible, to reach this person several days before the meeting is scheduled to begin. When it is actually under way, such people are ordinarily too busy to bother with anything so trivial as the problems of a master of ceremonies.

As a precautionary measure, you might check the information you get with someone else in the organization, just to make sure that the paid secretary isn't misrepresenting in order to grind an ax of his own. Do not use any names but inquire around casually and discover what reaction you get to the information given you. You may be saved a headache later on.

Specific Helps

You are now saying, "Enough of these generalities. What happens to me when I actually enter the banquet hall or dining room and am faced with the sea of white tablecloths? What happens then?"

Well, you will have those little cards in your pocket, on which you have prepared your advance material. You will have at least two sharp pencils stowed away. You will have extra cards or paper so you can make notes if required. You will have had a bath and your clothes will be neat, clean, and as good as you can afford.

The first thing you must do is to report to the committee chairman or person who arranged for your appearance, if he is available. He or she may be worrying about you. Under the stress of the occasion, he may be imagining that you have fallen under a heavy truck or are coming down with a severe case of pneumonia.

Next, you check the physical arrangements. Are you able to see everyone in the hall? Will they be able to see you? If not, make such arrangements as you can to remedy the situation after the food is served and before the program begins.

Check the sound system. Make sure you can be heard and find out if there are any idiosyncracies in the microphone set-up being provided. After taking these precautions, you are free to circulate among the guests to pick up such tidbits of information as may come your way.

From the foregoing, you can see that you cannot arrive five minutes before the company sits down to dinner and fulfill your obligation. It is essential that you be on hand from at least a half hour to forty-five minutes before the festivities are to begin. If you are early and no one is there, check such things as you can until the others arrive. Only in this way can you maintain that feeling of imperturbable calm which is part of your stock in trade as a master of ceremonies.

Earlier in this chapter, we called you a toastmaster. Since the point has come up, it might be well to clarify the distinction, if any, which lies between a toastmaster and a master of ceremonies. In the usage of the day, almost anyone who handles a program or who introduces people publicly is called a master of ceremonies, and the term can with propriety be used when referring to one who acts at a banquet. Strictly speaking, however, the master of ceremonies who appears when food is served should be known as a toastmaster. The question is not too important, but this is one of the original usages of the word, and it should be used whenever a luncheon or a dinner is part of the proceedings.

Some people may call you a chairman, but this term is scarcely correct. A chairman customarily serves at a more serious meeting. The toastmaster or master of ceremonies is primarily concerned, at least in this volume, with the presentation of entertainment in all its forms.

As either a toastmaster or master of ceremonies, it may be part of your duties to work with a chairman. If you are a stranger to the group, you can be introduced by someone who is a member, and he is regarded as the chairman.

Should you be appearing before a group which already knows you, such an introduction is not necessary. But if you are not known and are not introduced, valuable time may be lost at the beginning of the program, while everyone present tries to figure out who you are and why you are there. You should ask someone—the president or other officer—to introduce you to the assembled multitude in a few brief but well-chosen words.

Because you must, as quickly as possible, get on intimate terms with your audience, try to prevent this person from introducing you with such high-flown hyperbole that the audience is overawed instead of friendly. Should the chairman laud you to the skies, you can, of course, disparage everything he had to say, but such false modesty fools no one. Do not attempt it unless you can demolish the whole phony structure with one single laugh-provoking sentence. It is generally better to smile broadly, thank the chairman for his lovely introduction, and launch directly into what you have to say. You are lucky, though, if the chairman merely says that you are there and that you are going to be the master of ceremonies.

If you begin without benefit of introduction—and sometimes this is desirable—introduce yourself with a few words before you begin the program. It may ease the mental qualms of some poor soul who is wondering who you are.

Keep it simple. Something like the following might do, "Good evening, ladies and gentlemen. Doubtless I am a stranger to you. That may be a misfortune. On the other hand, you may be lucky, but my name is Erasmus Q. Fudnuk. I am associated in a vague way with one of the local banks, and I am here tonight to help you discover if some of the things we have for you add up to a certain sum in entertainment."

After the introduction, you can go on to a consideration of some of the other problems that you will meet in handling a banquet.

Group Singing

Occasionally you will be asked to lead the group in community singing before the actual program begins. Unless you have a natural facility for this sort of thing, your answer should be "No." When you are the master of ceremonies, it should not be necessary to double as a song leader, too. Do not imagine, however, that it takes any great voice to be able to function as a song leader. If your voice is loud and you have a great deal of enthusiasm, you will be able to get along very well.

However, it is a mistake to attempt to lead community singing without some kind of a song sheet, particularly with older people, many of whom will not be able to remember a song written in the last fifty years. The precaution of using a song sheet applies especially if you plan to lead a group in some of the more recent popular numbers. The words will have to be plainly mimeographed on sheets of paper and passed around, or you will have to have a song leader capable of teaching the words to a simple song as he goes along.

In any event, whether you do the job yourself or whether you have a song leader, vary the program with novelties, such as having the audience sing rounds or other stunt songs that might be interesting. Above all, do not continue the session too long. Before there is the slightest sign that the audience is tiring, stop the singing and go on with the rest of the program.

Remember that it is very incongruous to go from a jolly song program into something very serious or solemn, if you are both the song leader and the toastmaster. If you cannot accomplish the transition, have someone else lead the songs or dispense with them entirely.

Presentation of Gifts

At annual banquets and similar occasions, it is quite common for gifts or other mementoes to be presented to the departing officers. Here again, it will be better if someone else does the job. Less rarely will you be asked to make such a presentation, but if you are, suggest that a former officer of the organization be drafted to make such a presentation. It will look much better and sound much better than for an outsider to undertake the intimate task.

Keeping Attention

Frequently while you are conducting meetings, you will find that there are little disturbances in the audience with which it is difficult to cope. Someone will be whispering, or a little group off in one corner will be having a good time all by themselves.

There is very little you can do about a situation of this kind unless they disturb the rest of those present. Then, after looking at the speaker to make sure he, too, is conscious of the disturbance, you rap once or twice with your gavel and give the offenders a severe look.

If this fails to quell the disturbance, it may be necessary to dispatch someone from the head table by means of a note and ask him to tell the conversationalists to keep quiet. You will not meet with many situations of this kind, but it is well to know what to do with them when they occur.

The people at the head table have a great deal to do with the attitude of the audience toward the rest of the program. If they show an interest and are alert to what is being said, the chances are that the rest of the audience will have the same general attitude. Therefore it behooves everyone at the head table, including yourself, to look as interested as possible in the proceedings.

There is another source of disturbance for which the speaker himself is responsible. Often in an effort to avoid dullness he may bring exhibits of various kinds—pictures or rock samples, etc. During the course of his talk, he will pass these exhibits out into the audience for their inspection. This proceeding should not be tolerated. If you suspect that the speaker has exhibits of this nature, request that he place them on display before the program begins and make them available at the end. Otherwise they are a continual and unrewarding source of disorder during the course of the program.

Introducing Guests

Many times there will be special guests who will require introduction. They will be visiting officers from other organizations, former officers or other distinguished citizens who may have a special interest for the organization before which you are appearing. Check with the committee on arrangements beforehand. Learn who these people are and be prepared with as much information about them as you can get. Then in the few minutes that you have before dinner begins, go directly to the person involved and see if the information you have is correct.

This constant checking may seem like a good deal of nonsense, but at the average big banquet, under the best of conditions, you are going to make at least three errors in fact. Therefore it pays you to be very careful to see that you do not make any more.

When you do introduce your guests, try to do it all at once. Do not spread the various introductions throughout the evening. Save one particular space on your program and do these necessary amenities then. Not only will the audience applaud more heartily under this arrangement but there is less chance of slighting some important guest and injuring his dignity.

The Business End

After exercising such care, it would seem that the master of ceremonies is worth some extra consideration.

This book is addressed to the amateur—the person who has been asked to appear at some special function and is anxious to do a better-than-average job. Invariably, if you get through your first job without irretrievably ruining yourself, you will be asked to appear again, then again and again. Someone from this dinner or that banquet will remember you and, when arrangements are being made for another and totally unrelated affair, you will be called upon to serve. Unless you do something about it, you will be spending your time and energy in a lot of grueling work and will be getting very little in return.

Of course the answer is up to you. If you are a lawyer or an insurance man, such gratis appearances may be your cheapest form of advertising. But there comes a time, if you are fairly successful, when the demands for your services make it imperative that you charge for them.

Factors which go into the devising of a fee are your own reputation, the size of the town in which you live, the customary fee paid in similar circumstances, and the ability of the organization to pay. All things being equal, you are wisest when you charge all that the traffic will bear. Who knows when a different face, with a fresher slant and a newer line of jokes, will come to town and run you out of business?

For small dinners, of around fifty to a hundred and fifty people, twenty-five dollars is not unusual, although you may have to be satisfied with fifteen dollars or even ten. With larger groups, of from four to five hundred people, fifty to a hundred dollars is a very satisfactory fee. If you have a considerable reputation, if you are a well-known lawyer or newspaper man with the ability to keep an audience howling, you may be able to get much more—up to two hundred and fifty dollars. If you are able to command more than that, you are wasting your time in reading this book.

Actually you will get along much better if you charge for your services than if you appear for nothing before every group that asks you. People tend to appreciate you more if they have to pay for what you do, and you will not be bothered by being invited to waste your time on a lot of claptrap, if it is known that you charge for your work.

Here is where the services of a good agent prove valuable. The agent knows the going price for the type of thing you are doing and will be able to charge accordingly. For his end of the bargain, he will deduct ten or fifteen per cent from the fees you receive.

Occasionally even an agent will ask you to make a gratis appearance. Such a concession may be all right the first time, while he gets people acquainted with your work, or you can accept a smaller fee. After that, you should either get your full fee or stay home and listen to the radio. If eventually you get your full asking price, fine! If not, and you are finally forced to accept a lower figure, you will have a clearer idea of your true value as a master of ceremonies.

And where will you find an agent? Don't worry! If you appear at a banquet and turn out to be very good, one will immediately appear on your trail. That is, if the town in which you live is large enough to support a theatrical agent. If your town is too small, you will have to continue to conduct your business in your own way, and it may be just as well.

Even after you are established and can command good fees, there are jobs for which you will not expect to receive any remuneration. Church jobs are among them. Charity affairs at which no one else receives any pay can also be numbered among such performances, but if others receive pay for their services, you should be very niggardly about donating yours.

In no event, unless you so specify, should you be out of pocket for any expenses incurred through appearing at a charity function. If you pay your own transportation or have expenses in connection with the material you use, like ribbons cut in a magic act, you should be reimbursed. Otherwise you are making a double donation—one in time and one in money —and that is unfair. Do not hesitate to bring these matters to the attention of the committee before you appear, in fact before you even agree to appear. In that way, there can be no possibility of a misunderstanding afterwards.

You yourself will have to decide how many charity entertainments you can handle in a year. After you have decided, it should be very difficult for anyone to force you to reconsider your plans. If you can find an excuse or plead other business, you will get along much better than if you appear everywhere working for nothing.

Even when you do work for nothing, it does not pay to place yourself at the mercy of everyone who chooses to demand your services. Place a premium on those services, make them hard to get, and they will be much more appreciated when they are given.

Some Good Ideas

If you are going to be worth your pay as a master of ceremonies, there are a few things that you ought to know which are not generally available in courses of speech instruction but which you have to learn the hard way. Some of these are as follows. When movies or lantern slides are shown, no one ever thinks to have a man available to turn off the lights at the proper time. See that this is done and that the person is properly rehearsed so that he turns off the correct lights without at the same time turning off the projector and the ventilating fan in the furnace room.

The seats provided in the average banquet hall are one of the afflictions of the human race. They are folding chairs of hard metal to which the human frame can accommodate itself only with a great deal of difficulty. If the meeting is going to be longer than will permit people to sit in such chairs with comfort, call a recess. At banquets, call a recess between the dinner and the start of the program or before the appearance of the principal speaker. In no case, have an audience sit longer than an hour and a half without some sort of relief. These recess periods should be no longer than necessary—three to five minutes will generally suffice—but they will help considerably if the program is unusually long.

Do not permit an audience to remain too hot or too cold without trying to do something about it. If a room is too hot, ask that windows be opened or that ventilation be provided. If too cold, make sure that heat is supplied. At the same time, see to it, whenever possible, that no one sits in an unavoidable draft. An uncomfortable audience is a poor audience, and there is little point in handicapping yourself by appearing before an audience that is too uncomfortable to appreciate your efforts.

Remember that banquet halls and auditoriums are kept cooler than normal before the arrival of an audience. After they begin to fill up, the temperature rises. A temperature of seventy degrees in an auditorium before the audience arrives will prove to be suffocating after it is filled with people. A temperature of sixty-five degrees is more nearly right before the audience arrives, although this reading will vary with the size and construction of the hall. If the ceiling is low, sixty degrees may be more nearly right.

Another idea has to do with the speaker who is running overtime. Before any speaking program, try to have a definite understanding with everyone as to how much time is to be taken by each individual speaker. If a speaker exceeds his limit by only two or three minutes, no great harm is done. But the speaker who takes the bit in his teeth and keeps on running, regardless of the fact that he may be saying nothing, has to be stopped.

If the speaker is badly overtime and shows no hint of winding up his remarks, you have no choice but to pass him a note reading in big capital letters, "YOU ARE RUNNING OVERTIME!" Should he then continue to ignore all the rules of fairness and courtesy—and he will unless he has honestly lost track of the time—you have the unpleasant duty of rising at an appropriate moment, leading the applause as though he were finished, thanking him for his remarks, and then going on to introduce the next speaker.

The person to whom this is done will hate you, but you cannot waste the time of everyone present and exhaust the patience of your other speakers as well. Capable speakers almost invariably ask you how much time is available and strive mightily to keep within those limits. It is the incapable ones who cause you all the trouble.

CHAPTER ELEVEN

THE SERIOUS MEETING

Until now, the master of ceremonies has been considered as a species of entertainer or as a channel through which information flows to an audience. When he is conducting a serious meeting, the same classification applies. The difference lies in a change of emphasis.

Even though you do a good job as an entertaining type of master of ceremonies, you may never be asked to perform at a serious meeting. Someone better known but perhaps less capable will be asked instead. Should the job fall to your lot, however, there are a few basic rules which are essential.

In the first place, the question of tempo is not particularly important. You do not have to keep things humming at quite the same pace that you do when entertainment alone is being presented. Even so, no meeting should ever be permitted to drag.

Second, at a serious meeting, you generally avoid humor, although there are occasions when it is not out of place. Keep your introductions simpler and more to the point than in the entertainment program and keep them as short as possible. You will not have to sell as hard as when you are trying to put across a program of simple entertainment; at least you will do it in a different way. Other than that, you will follow the basic rules which have been laid down in Chapters Two and Three.

For instance, if you have a speaker who is very well known, there is no harm in seeing to it that the audience becomes acquainted with that fact. Build him up a little. Although you may dwell only on those things which are pertinent to the meeting and though you may do it with more dignity and reserve than you employ in presenting an entertainment program, there is no reason why you should not make every effort to see that the program is properly appreciated.

As in everything else, taste must be the final guide. A little experience plus an alertness to the needs of your audience will enable you to present almost anything at any meeting.

Sales Meetings

There are really only two kinds of sales meetings: those which are deadly dull and those which are so filled with furious activity that no one can tell what they are all about.

Occasionally, however, an exceptionally intelligent management will call in an outsider to act as a master of ceremonies, and he might be you. When this happens, you sit down with those in charge and try to figure out what they are trying to accomplish by the meeting. Invariably the object will be more sales, but there may be many and devious routes by which they hope to achieve this objective.

Your job is to take note of the various items on the agenda and then, within the framework of the over-all objective, try to present them in such a way that they have a little freshness and originality. Frankly the job will not be too difficult because, since you yourself are not already a member of the organization, your mere presence will add a note of the unusual.

Frequently, however, when you are called upon to perform at this kind of meeting, you will find that someone—a junior executive, no doubt—will already have very definite ideas as to how it should be done. He will insist that everything be done his way. When that happens, you have little choice but to bow out. There is no sense in ruining your reputation and, besides, you were called in to give things a fresh slant. If someone insists that they be done in the same old way, very little has been accomplished.

Certainly when you appear before a private commercial organization, you should expect to get paid, unless in return you hope to sell them a fat contract. Even then you should look at free performances of this kind with a jaundiced eye.

That junior executive, mentioned earlier, may see to it that you never get the contract anyway.

Of course, if you yourself work for the company conducting the meetings, there will be very little you can do about it one way or the other. You will have to do exactly what your employer tells you, and you may have to listen to his wife. However, there is one advantage to giving your own individual little touches. If they go over, you may be able to persuade the boss that he thought of them himself and, in that way, both of you will be much happier.

As a matter of fact, there are only two types of sales meetings: those which are given for members of the same organization and those which are given for a number of outside dealers who are ostensibly members of their own organizations. The meetings of the first type are generally smaller, and they come at all hours of the day or night. In conducting them, you have to follow a pattern rather closely. The meetings of the second type, on the other hand, are usually presented in a good-sized convention hall, sometimes on a very large scale. Here you will be permitted a little more leeway in the presentation of your material.

At a sales meeting, you should strive to inject as many personal touches as you possibly can. Use the house jokes, if you want to call them that—trade humor which is familiar to everyone in the particular business involved. Use private company jokes. Localize your material in any way you can, even by inserting the names of those present into some of your jokes. Capably done such tactics can do a great deal to rescue the average sales meeting from the incipient rigor mortis which usually attacks it.

Campaign Dinners

Campaign dinners are akin to sales meetings in that they seek to engender enthusiasm in order that some mammoth goal may be achieved. Fund drives are a typical example. The faults of the average sales meeting are present here, only they are multiplied because, instead of being paid to sit and suffer, the audience is customarily donating its services.

There are three objectives in any meeting of this type: Explain the goal, outline the methods by which it is to be achieved, and send the members of the audience on their way. Do not kill the initial impetus which brought the volunteers to the meeting in the first place. Be brief!

Introductions at a meeting of this kind should be short and to the point, without a wasted word. At a drive breakfast especially, any audience is bound to resent an effort to tell a long and involved story. Get on with it! Save such efforts for the folks at home.

Observances and Dedications

In many communities, especially the smaller ones, the national holidays are the occasion for a considerable observance, far more than in the larger cities. The program is held out of doors in a public park. The band plays and a speaker is imported from as far away as possible. Sometimes a new church, a new school, or a farmer's elevator is dedicated, thus offering another opportunity for a master of ceremonies to peddle his wares.

Although many of the rules mentioned earlier apply here as well, there is a decided change in emphasis. The audience comes to the meeting expecting a serious if not profound treatment of whatever is being done and will be disappointed if it is not forthcoming.

It is here that the modern emphasis on informality has done its greatest damage. Speakers are too prone to rise, stumble half apologetically through some little speech, and then sit down as though everything possible had been said. It has become unfashionable to appeal to the simpler sentiments like patriotism or to treat a serious subject in any but the most cursory fashion.

Seldom does it hurt to appeal to the basic values and, if a subject demands serious treatment, that is the kind which should be given. Pomposity is out, but a serious thought, well phrased and sincerely spoken, is acceptable at any time.

You must, at the start, make a simple statement as to why

the meeting is being held. With this exception, it is not the function of the master of ceremonies to dilate lengthily upon the subject in hand. At a Memorial Day exercises, for instance, he should not give a long-winded dissertation on the subject of Memorial Day, but should say simply that these are the annual exercises conducted in honor of our soldier dead by whatever veterans' organization is in charge of the service. The work of further recognizing the holiday's significance should be left to the other speakers on the program, though if anything essential is left unsaid, the master of ceremonies can insert it at a convenient point before the end.

Ordinarily, however, the exact reverse is true. There is too much repetition. All the speakers say essentially the same thing. This tendency should be watched carefully. Even though you had planned to make some very choice references to the occasion, if the same approach is made by someone else, cut it ruthlessly from your own remarks. The very next speaker may have the same idea, and by the time the audience has heard the same thought expressed by two or three different speakers, they may be driven quietly mad. As the master of ceremonies, you should avoid using the same kind of general expressions that are apt to be used by anyone else on the program. In other words, you should take care not to steal anyone else's material.

On any serious program, it is doubly important that everything be checked beforehand—speakers' stand, microphones, chairs, and what not—because, if anything goes wrong, it is certain to have a detrimental effect upon the spirit of the meeting. It is not always essential that you do this work yourself, but you should make certain that it will be done. Nothing, for instance, is more embarrassing than to have a group of people file solemnly upon a platform, only to discover that there are not enough chairs to go around.

Many times those faced with the problem of assembling a holiday or dedicatory program are at a loss as to how to proceed. Since most of these programs are not strikingly original in either arrangement or content, it helps to procure samples from other communities where programs of a similar nature have already been presented. By changing such a program to meet local conditions, by making various other adaptations, and by adding such original touches as you can, you may be able to save yourself much work and worry. At the same time, you should not close your mind to a new idea, if one comes along.

Patriotic exercises are frequently better if they follow the same general pattern from year to year. It is very hard to improve, for instance, on the pledge of allegiance to the flag. If you follow some sort of traditional ceremony, you are more likely to achieve the desired result than if you strike out blindly upon untried pathways, merely to achieve some effect conspicuously new or different. Use originality when you can, but in the basic elements stick rather close to the essentials. It is most unwise to trifle with those traditional institutions whose principal strength lies in their unchanging sameness. When you give the pledge to the flag, for instance, do not try to add decorative touches that may detract from its principal purpose. Keep it simple, and you are certain to achieve the results you seek.

At dedication exercises, it is customary to mark the event as an historical milestone in the growth of the town, the community, or what you will. The old is contrasted with the new, and a beacon light is pointed down the road leading to a new and brighter tomorrow.

It is important, at such ceremonies, to see that everyone who had anything at all to do with the project receive some sort of recognition. If a school building is being dedicated, recognition should be given to the school board, the architect, the superintendent of schools, the men who actually did the building, and anyone else who might have conceivably had anything to do with the enterprise. The recognition may be verbal, or the persons recognized may be permitted to take a bow.

At all such functions, there is little or no opportunity to check procedure beforehand. At least, there is little opportunity for rehearsal. It is important then that everyone understand exactly what is expected of him. To that end, have the committee print or mimeograph a schedule of events, together with any special instructions that might be for the benefit of those participating. See that everyone gets a copy. By this precaution, you eliminate the necessity of having the participants come to you to find out what is going on. Through keeping your peace of mind in this manner, you are better able to do an acceptable job yourself.

Finally, at any dedication exercise or patriotic ceremony, be sincere. Facetiousness or a tongue-in-the-cheek attitude will get you nowhere. If you appeal to the spirit of patriotism or for a better tomorrow, you had better mean it or you will find your audience slowly drifting away. The people who attend such ceremonies are not especially sophisticated or else they are not in a sophisticated mood. You will be better off if you do what you have to do in a spirit of simple sincerity.

Memorial Services

With surprising frequency you may be asked to officiate at memorial services to honor friends or civic leaders who have passed away. Such services are usually presented by a group of persons who expound briefly upon various phases in the life of the one who has died. It is not customary when introducing these people to do any more than give the name.

The master of ceremonies begins the service with a brief biography of the person for whom the service is being held. He then introduces the first speaker simply, by name and subject. For instance, he says, "John Smith will now tell you about his achievements as a member of the Board of Governors of the orphans' home." Each speaker then introduces the next person in much the same manner. At the end, the master of ceremonies may appear again, to inform those present where to sign the memorial register or how they can make memorial gifts on behalf of the deceased.

Forums and Debates

There are times when nothing is more deadly than a forum or a debate. Then, suddenly for reasons unknown to the mind of man, these performances regain their popularity and you cannot round a familiar corner without running into a couple of speakers expounding upon one of their favorite subjects.

When introducing a forum, you should reach an agreement with the speakers beforehand as to the exact meaning of the subject. Then you can let the audience know what they are in for right at the start and save the time of the speakers who follow. They will not have to explain the subject or waste time that might better be devoted to opposing arguments.

To achieve this end, you will have to discover what aspects of any subject your speakers wish to discuss. For instance, in the case of "Wheat Marketing Problems Today," you will not want to waste time explaining the difficulties of getting the wheat to the country elevator when the big problem is a shortage of railroad cars to haul the grain from the elevators to the terminal markets.

You will thus begin your introduction by narrowing the subject down to the particular phase involved, explain its timeliness, and then go on with a discussion of the qualifications of your speakers to handle the topic. At the same time, be careful to give approximately an equal opportunity to each speaker, or you may be accused of partiality.

In debates, besides the points outlined above, you may have to keep time, although someone else should be delegated to handle this job whenever possible. If you have to keep time—and often there is no one else available—make sure that you have a good watch, preferably a stop watch, and find out beforehand how much time has been alloted for the presentation of arguments. Ten, fifteen, or twenty minutes are customarily allowed for the presentation of initial arguments while five minutes, or even less, are allowed for rebuttal. The affirmative side usually speaks first.

With either the forum, which is simply a group of speakers talking about the same general subject, or with the debate, an opportunity for questions is often provided at the end. It is part of your job as chairman to see that fairness is exercised in this department as well. Insist that only one question be asked at a time and that all are given a chance to be heard.

The moment there is a lag, rap the gavel and bring the meeting to an end.

The Broadcast Meeting

It frequently happens that a portion of the meeting where you are officiating will be broadcast, perhaps, even televised. You should therefore have more than a vague notion of how to carry on under the circumstances.

The problem lies in timing the proceedings so you reach the part to be broadcast on the nose, which is broadcast parlance for the exact time. It is not so difficult as it sounds.

Since only the principal speaker may be heard over the air, you must arrange the program in such a way that there is a reasonable degree of flexibility in those moments immediately preceding the part to be broadcast. If time runs short, there must be something to delete. If not, and you must stall along until the hour of the broadcast, there should be something that you can use to fill up the interval of time. It would be well for you to have a number of short items which can be eliminated or not just before the broadcast, depending upon the circumstances.

Such a procedure, however, is not always practicable and, since you will not want to cut anyone off in the middle of a speech or in a song, you should be prepared to fill in the time yourself, either with a couple of stories or with a number of short announcements, if you have them. In a pinch, you can even tell your audience that you are waiting for the time of the broadcast and invite them to enjoy one another's company until the great moment arrives. You should not take this step, however, unless it is absolutely necessary, as it detracts from the smoothness of the performance and allows the bare bones to show. Besides, asking the audience to wait until the actual moment of the broadcast may prove vaguely irritating to those present and spoil some of the applause and laughter that you might otherwise get. Therefore it behooves you to slide into the broadcast portions of any meeting as smoothly as possible.

Normally you will get every co-operation from the station personnel. Two people will handle the show—an announcer and an engineer. In some cases, a production man will come along, too, in which instance you will work directly with him instead of the announcer.

Check with either one or the other to find out whether you will introduce the speaker on the air or whether the announcer will. The decision in this matter will be dictated somewhat by the amount of time required by the speaker, but there are several ways in which the situation can be handled.

One way is for the announcer, off stage if possible, to introduce you. You introduce the speaker, and he launches into his talk. If you take the other way, you may not even appear on the air at all. If it seems that the speaker is going to require all the time available, it may be best if you introduce him first to the live audience before you go on the air. Then after this introduction the announcer introduces him to the air audience, either in front of the live audience or off stage. Your sole function will be to see to it that he gets a round of applause when he rises to his feet.

Since broadcast time is rather valuable, you may not wish to take a great deal of time or make a great ado when you introduce the speaker on the air. Yet if you feel that a more complete introduction is desirable, with a live audience present, the best way to handle such a situation is to introduce the speaker to the live audience before the broadcast begins, explaining that you are merely introducing him in this way so that those present can get better acquainted with him. Then, after you have received your introduction from the station announcer, go ahead and make your shorter, more informal introduction on the air. The speaker rises to the tide of applause which was withheld the first time the introduction was made.

Properly done, this method of making the introduction is a way of complimenting the audience for their sagacity in being present on such an auspicious occasion and removes the sting of any inconvenience which may have been caused by the broadcast.

Your principal worry is to make sure that you do not repeat information which has been given to the radio audience by the announcer. For instance, it is not necessary to tell the listeners that the broadcast is coming to them from the Palm Room of the Grand Central Hotel. That information should be handled by the station announcer. You should stick to the more explicit or personal items of information which cannot be given in the formal opening and closing to the program.

Occasionally you will meet speakers experienced enough to lengthen or shorten their speeches to fit the amount of air time available, but these are exceptional. Again, your speaker may broadcast only a part of his speech and continue with the live audience after the program has been taken off the air. It all depends on the ramifications of the situation, and they are many.

Leaving the air on time at the end is much simpler than beginning the broadcast because, should the speech run too long, the station will cut the speaker off the air anyway, unless he is unusually important. If the speech runs short, the announcer will turn the program back to the studios where a musical fill will be provided till station break time.

Regardless of how it is done, however, an effort should be made to have the broadcast "time out," i. e., fill the allotted space without hurry at the end.

To assist you in this respect, the station announcer should give you hand signals indicating the number of minutes left on the broadcast. Five fingers held up mean five minutes. One upraised finger indicates one minute, and on this signal the speaker had better start preparing to wind up his end of the program, although it is surprising, at times, how much can be said in a minute. One half a finger held up (bent at the knuckle) indicates that there is only one half a minute remaining on the air and warns the speaker that his time is running out.

Time should be calculated on the basis of the actual number of minutes remaining to the speaker and not on the amount of time left for the entire program. The station announcer must have time for a concluding announcement at the end of the broadcast. A good watch, lying beside you on the table, can be of immeasurable assistance in keeping track of the time, but hand signals from the station personnel can be very reassuring indeed.

If you are speaking before the broadcast in order to fill in time, the announcer can assist you with unobtrusive hand signals given from the side or rear of the hall. Thus you will know how much time is remaining until the broadcast begins without having to glance constantly at your watch. When the cue comes to begin, the announcer should give you a hand signal as well as a vocal cue, in the event that you have any difficulty hearing in what might be a crowded hall. With the aid of these signals, you can gauge yourself more accurately and thus do a neater job of switching from the live part of the program into the broadcast.

Rarely will radio or television people arrive on the scene much before the time of the broadcast. You may have to do your checking with them while the meeting is acually in progress, although this procedure should be avoided if at all possible. If you are the least bit uncertain as to how the broadcast is to be handled, go to the studio beforehand and get the necessary information.

Ordinarily the announcer or production people handling such broadcasts will have had a great deal of experience and will be able to tell you in a few words what is wanted. The broadcast is their responsibility, and they should be able to get you on and off the air without a great deal of difficulty.

Only rarely as a master of ceremonies will you be expected to say anything at the conclusion of a broadcast. Your worries are over the moment the principal speaker starts on the air. You will, however, thank the speaker at the end for the benefit of the live audience and carry on with any parts of the program that are left after the broadcast.

As a final hint, if the broadcast microphone is left on the table before you, do not say anything that might be considered offensive by the air audience unless you are absolutely sure that the instrument has been disconnected. Jocular masters of ceremonies have done themselves no good in this way by making remarks that might be misconstrued, although experienced radio people will rarely leave a live microphone standing idly about. Usually the engineer turns off the switch the moment the microphone is no longer in use.

Invocations and Dedications

No one is quite so disturbed as the master of ceremonies who suddenly finds himself faced with the necessity of introducing a rabbi, a priest, or a minister for an unfamiliar religious ritual, when he has not done so before.

At formal exercises, dedications, and the like, it is quite common to have a religious leader invoke the presence of God at the beginning of the ceremony and to ask His blessing at the end. Many times a different person will appear for each of the two rituals, in which event it is necessary to have the correct name and form of address for each of them.

If they are unknown to the audience, as is often the case, it will be a courtesy to give enough about the man so that the audience knows who is speaking. The rest of the procedure is fairly simple. For the one ritual say, "We will rise for the invocation pronounced by Father———— (give full name) of the Church of the Blessed Sacrament." For the other, "We will rise for a benediction by Rabbi ———— (give full name) of the Beth El Synagogue."

If the religious person should be from out of town or if the audience should be largely composed of outsiders, it does no harm to give the location of the man's church. Before an out-of-town convention, for instance, those attending might like to know that the rabbi, priest, or minister is a local man. Use as few words as possible. Give the man's correct title, say what he is going to do, and give his church affiliation and its location.

Normally, it is best if you ask the audience to rise. There

will be less confusion if the situation is handled in this way, and the churchman will not have to make the usual gesture, which may be misunderstood by some of those present.

Patriotic Ceremony

Much the same methods are pursued when you are asking the audience to participate in a patriotic service. Keep the wordage to a minimum. The presumption is that nothing you can say will add anything to the spirit of the occasion. Say simply, "Miss Lucy Doe, accompanied by Peter Roe, will lead us in the singing of 'The Star Spangled Banner' " or "Gladys Roe, of the Roosevelt School, will lead us in the pledge to the flag."

If a child has been selected to lead the pledge to the flag because of some meritorious achievement, it is permissible to include this fact in the introduction, but it should be done tactfully. You might say, for instance, "Richard Smith, winner of this year's Leadership Prize at the Whittier School, will lead us in the pledge of allegiance to the flag."

Terms of Address

When you are before the public, you will be called upon to introduce public figures and to speak to them more or less informally in the course of debates or round-table discussions. To avoid embarrassment, you should have a reasonable familiarity with the correct terms of address used for many offices.

There is customarily both a formal and an informal mode of address, although the distinction is not always followed. Governors, for instance, are formally introduced as "His Excellency, the Honorable Wilford Fudnuk, Governor of the State of Alarm." But such an introduction before many audiences would only provoke titters and probably ruin the political prospects of the Governor forever. Therefore a sort of compromise is reached. It is much safer, in some circumstances, to introduce the Governor in the following terms: "The Honorable Wilford Fudnuk, Governor of the State of Alarm. Governor Fudnuk."

The same formula can be applied to most holders of public offices above the rank of mayor, up to and including the President of the United States, who is generally introduced as The President of the United States and nothing more. It is assumed that anyone who does not know the name of the President of the United States is too ignorant to deserve any consideration. The Vice President of the United States is properly introduced as The Honorable Blank Blank, Vice President of the United States.

Cabinet officers are also referred to as The Honorable, with the name followed by the office; for example: "The Honorable Joe Blow, Secretary of the Interior." Informally such officers are addressed as Mr. Secretary.

In the two legislative branches of the national government, members of the lower house are addressed informally as Congressman. Those in the upper are called Senator, although the title, The Honorable, is most generally applied in conjunction with the full name. The following is an example of the formal introduction: "The Honorable Ghastly P. Fudnuk, Member of Congress from the State of Alarm." In introducing a member of Congress, however, it is sometimes advisable to give the number of his congressional district and, in the case of both senators and representatives, to give the party designation.

The title, His Excellency, though frowned upon when used in reference to an American Governor, seems to pass muster when used in connection with an ambassador or a minister, probably because these diplomats have spent so much time on foreign soil that they are presumed to be a little bit queer anyway. The correct form is His Excellency, the Honorable Gerald Fudnuk, American Ambassador to Brazil. The same formula applies if he is only a minister. Informally the one is addressed as Mr. Ambassador, the other as Mr. Minister.

Officers of courts are also addressed as The Honorable, with the name followed by the title of the office; for example: The Honorable Legal Eagle, Chief Justice of the Supreme Court." The Chief Justice of the United States, for some reason, is known only as The Chief Justice of the Supreme Court, without the name of the country, while an associate justice is known as The Honorable Junior Eagle, Justice, Supreme Court of the United States.

Judicial officers of the various states are handled in much the same fashion, with the head of the state supreme court being addressed as Chief Justice of the Supreme Court and a fellow worker as Associate Justice of the Supreme Court. Informally they can all be addressed as Mr. Justice Eagle.

Perhaps you are wondering why it is necessary to make such a fetish of using the correct term of address. You may never be called upon, you say, to use any of these titles. Don't you believe it! You may very well be called upon to introduce the principal speaker at a political meeting and, since there is seldom time to check on such things beforehand, it is well to have, at least, a working knowledge of the rules. Not only will you be able to make a better impression as a knowing fellow, but you will also run less risk of creating offense among the partisans of the man involved. He may not take offense if you miscall his name and title, but his local friends may, and that is where your problem lies. There is no point in doing the job at all if you are going to irritate some people by lack of a single bit of knowledge.

Most state officers, as indicated earlier in the example about the Governor, are introduced as The Honorable. Much of the time, during informal conversation, they are addressed as Governor, Senator, or whatever the title may be. Here, as in other instances, the title is most often used in conjunction with the man's name, as in the following question, "Governor Jones, what do you think of this year's crop of potatoes?"

In the lower ranking orders of city or county officers, the title, The Honorable, is not often used, except with the mayor, who is known as His Honor, the Mayor. Informally he can be addressed as Your Honor, as Mayor Jones, or simply as Mayor.

The same general routine applies with other city and county officials such as commissioners, sheriffs, or chiefs of police. It is quite all right to address the Chief of Police as Chief or as Chief Fudnuk.

As a matter of fact, on the lower levels, many officials are apt to look with displeasure on any attempt to be too formal in the mode of address. They feel that they may be made to appear snobbish and thus offend some of the voters. You will have to use good judgment in this respect. When introducing the Chief of Police, for instance, it may be all right to abide by his desire to appear as just "another one of the boys." At the same time, you will have to show a certain respect for the office in order to maintain your own dignity. A happy medium will doubtless prove best.

Educational honors are handled in much the same fashion except that the term, The Honorable, is used only when the bearer has served honorably in an elective or appointive governmental office. Titles you will meet in this field are Chancellor, Doctor, President, Dean, and Professor or Associate Professor. Some of these people may have two titles, as with the professor who is also a doctor, in which case he is announced as Dr. Ezra Peabody, Professor of Comparative Zoology at Pumpkinhead University.

In the lower areas of the educational world, the term, Mister, is usually sufficient, when combined with a description of the office, as in the following sample introductions: "Mr. Robert Smith, Principal of West Side High School" and "Miss Henrietta Fudnuk, Superintendent of Schools in East Tadpole, Illinois."

The churches, too, have their customary forms of address which should be observed.

In the Catholic Church, cardinals are known as His Eminence ———— (give first name) Cardinal ———— (give last name); they are addressed as Your Eminence. Archbishops and bishops are known as The Most Reverend ———— (give full name). Archbishops are addressed as Your Grace. Although both archbishops and bishops can be addressed as Your Excellency, during informal conversation, they can also be addressed as Archbishop ———— (give last name) or Bishop ———— (give last name). Monsignori are known as The Right Reverend Monsignor ———— (give full name) or The Very Reverend Monsignor ———— (give full name). Informally, the are addressed as Monsignor. Priest are known as The Reverend ———— (give full name) or The Very Reverend ———— (give full name) and addressed as Father.

The Protestant Episcopal Church also has a group of clergy for whom there are varied forms of address. The titles are Bishop, Archdeacon, Canon, and Rector. Bishops are known as The Right Reverend John B. Jones and addressed as Bishop Jones. Archdeacons are known as The Venerable John R. Jones and addressed as Archdeacon Jones. Deans are known as The Very Reverend John Q. Jones and addressed as Dean Jones, while canons and rectors are known as The Reverend John P. Jones and addressed as either Canon Jones or Reverend Jones.

Remember that members of the clergy in most denominations, unless otherwise designated, should be introduced as The Reverend ———— (give full name), with the exception of the Jewish faith, in which the correct title is Rabbi or sometimes Doctor. Informally these men or, on occasion, women, can be addressed as Reverend Blank, Doctor Blank or, in the case of Lutheran churches, as Pastor Blank.

Under many circumstances, it is exceedingly difficult to ask some of these people the correct form of address, but if you are uncertain it is better to ask than to make a mistake. Make sure, too, that you have all of the title. Church officers may have place designations as well as particular titles. Bishops, for instance, are bishops of a certain area—a town or a city. Often a churchman may serve in an office which is just as important as the other parts of his title. A simple priest may be the vice-chancellor of a diocese.

By asking for this information, you will not only avoid the possibility of slighting an important visitor but also members of your audience who may have a special interest in seeing to it that the man is correctly introduced. You may also avoid getting a public correction, than which there is nothing more embarrassing. In this matter, as in other things, always be sure before you go ahead.

CHAPTER TWELVE

SOME FINAL WORDS

You will shortly discover, after your first experience as a master of ceremonies, that there are certain aspects of the average speech situation which are not exactly as advertised. For instance, many people will tell you, after your first uncertain trial, that you will improve with age. You may do so, but you may get worse. It depends on the mental attitude you have when viewing your work.

If you look at it coldly from the strictly professional point of view, if you try to see where mistakes were made, you may improve. If, on the other hand, you regard each golden word as divinely inspired, you are more apt to wind up as an opinionated old fossil of no particular value to anyone.

A certain amount of helpful criticism from a friend or relative in the audience may prove to be a good thing. Your husband or wife can tell you if you are repeating a word or a phrase too many times or if you are employing an awkward gesture. But the effort toward self improvement is not the only thing to keep in mind if you are appearing regularly before the public.

The first thing you must realize is that all audiences are not the same. There are psychological factors involved which may make any audience different from the one that went before it. Sudden storms or even a change in the weather may affect an audience in a way that you will be able to detect after you have had a little experience. A Monday night audience is different from a Friday night audience and so on.

As you go along you will learn how to take these factors into account and guide yourself accordingly. It may be even advisable to refer to the thing which is agitating the audience, like the sudden rainstorm, and thus bring the hidden thought to the surface, where it can be more easily forgotten.

In such a situation, you will often discover that the direct approach frequently pays the biggest dividends. For instance, should a fire engine go by, it will be better to refer to the screaming siren rather than ignore it. By so doing, you bring the audience's attention back to you rather than allow it to wander after the retreating fire engine down the street.

By sensing these inner disturbances in the minds of your audience, you may be able to prevent your own work from going flat and stale—which might happen if you ignore a basic factor like rain or cold or an exceptionally heavy snowstorm.

As a matter of fact, you will discover, after you have appeared a number of times, that there are occasions when, regardless of the effort put forth, you do not seem to "click." Perhaps, you yourself are not up to par. The audience may not be aware that anything is amiss but you do not feel that you are doing your best. At other times, there may be a genuine letdown, and nothing you can do seems to arouse the audience.

Unless they happen too often, these lapses are nothing to worry about. If you worry, you are not apt to shake them. If instead you go ahead and do the best you can, you may be able to improve the situation and thus shorten the period when everything seems to be down in the doldrums.

There are a number of factors which can make for such a condition. In the first place, your own health may not be all that it should be. You may be lacking sleep, or your energy may be low for a variety of other reasons. Your audience may have eaten too heavy a dinner. They may react too slowly because the hall is too hot or because it is too cold.

People themselves are inherently different. What seems funny to one may not move another to laughter, although there are subjects of universal appeal which seem to get a reaction from almost any kind of audience, though in varying degree.

You must make up your mind also that in spite of every thing you can do, you are not going to please every person in every audience. After any appearance, you may have a visit from some well-meaning but brutally frank individual who may criticize either you or your work, sometimes most unfairly. Listen to him gracefully. If he offers something you can use, try it and see how it works. If not, write the experience off as something you must undergo if you are going to appear before the public.

Cranks there are aplenty, and if you are either hired or invited to act as master of ceremonies before some club or group of which such a one is a member, you will simply have to put up with him. However, with practice you will become adept at avoiding such pests in every way possible. A good method is to keep a pencil and paper at hand. Then when the crank approaches or begins to bore you to tears, act as though you suddenly saw someone across the room and hurry over under the pretense that you have to make notes on what he tells you. The average crank will not wake up to this subterfuge until you have done it to the same person at least two or three times. Even then, he will not be able to figure out why you did it.

Cranks are people who have axes to grind or who wish to tell you the story of their lives. You cannot permit yourself to get bored with them because it will interfere with the quality of your work. You have to keep a free mind when appearing before an audience, and you cannot do it if you are worrying about some crackpot who insists on hanging about your neck and telling you all his troubles. This attitude may seem ruthless, but what else can you do?

When you are appearing before a club or a group of which you are not a member, you will have to adopt a thoroughly professional attitude. That shapely blonde off in one corner will have to be ignored, as will the man who might be able to do you a business favor. You will have to treat all comers alike. The most crashing bore and the person with something to say will have to be treated with equal consideration. Since the toastmaster frequently mixes with a dinner audience before and after the event, you will have to cultivate a considerable amount of poise. But the results may be worth the effort.

One worry is stage fright. Stage fright is self-consciousness, and self-consciousness is thinking about one's self. If you have properly prepared your material, stage fright should not be too big a factor. Generally stage fright disappears after you launch into your work and the returns begin to come in. There are, however, a number of little tricks which may help you to circumvent stage fright in its more virulent forms.

The first of these is to cultivate a sense of well-being. If you are rested and your nerves are calm, you will get along much better than if you are teetering along the ragged edge of a nervous attack. This sense of well-being can be cultivated by a number of factors which are totally unrelated to the job in hand.

A good warm bath, taken at a leisurely pace, will work wonders. Clean clothes and a general feeling of spruceness from the skin out are of immense help. A manicure and fresh shave, if you are a man, and a facial, if you are a woman, will add a feeling of re-assuring self-confidence. The tonic effect of a good mild cologne will do a surprising amount of good. All these things can contribute something to your mental well-being.

If you arrive at the job feeling well and looking well, you are much better prepared to survive the ordeal than you are if you throw yourself together with an unskilled hand and arrive breathlessly at the last possible moment.

Of course, you will never get over stage fright completely. Perhaps you never should. It is a whip that drives you on to do your best. It should be possible, however, to appear before an audience without completely lacerating your nerves.

Even if you conquer stage fright, there is one more factor which ought to be kept in mind. If your audience is unable to hear or understand you, you will not be successful, regardless of what you say.

You probably remember the story of the Greek orator who practised clear speaking by placing pebbles in his mouth while he talked. You may not have to go quite that far, but you should take care that your words are distinct and well formed. Slovenly speech is no attribute of a good master of ceremonies.

Avoid pronunciations like "git" for "get" or "jist" for "just." Use a dictionary. Try not to be affected, but at the same time speak a good workmanlike brand of English or American, if you prefer to call it that. Your audience may not appreciate directly what you are doing, but you yourself will get more pleasure out of your work if you are consciously trying to do the best job possible.

Speaking of pleasure, there is that little matter of collecting your pay. If you work through an agent or booker, that problem will be handled for you by him or her, as the case may be, and you will get a check at a later date, minus the usual commission. If, however, you book directly, it is customary at most dinners or meetings to pay the master of ceremonies beforehand. Sometimes the secretary or treasurer will simply hand you a check. At other times, the money or the check will be enclosed in an envelope which you will carefully tuck into your pocket.

On the other hand, you may not be paid until the meeting is over, in which case it is not at all amiss to remind the person involved that you have some money coming. Many people regard a worker in the arts as one who should probably work for nothing, if it can be arranged. You therefore have to remind your employers about payment if it seems to be forgotten. Say something like the following, "I presume you would like my address so you can send the check." After such a reminder, the check will usually be forthcoming at once; but, if not, send a bill immediately. Even the most conscientious secretary may dread paying the fiddlers when the party is a long time over. Stress prompt payment, or you may not get the money at all.

Finally remember that when you step in front of an audience, the people of that audience want to like you. They want to laugh. They want to have fun. If you keep that fact in mind, you will get along much better than if you regard each appearance as something of an ordeal.

As a matter of fact, very few speakers have been shot to death by an audience, at least not for speaking. Take it calmly.

Being a master of ceremonies is like almost anything else. It is the art of getting along with people. If you can do that and, at the same time, preserve your own self-respect, you are not likely to have any trouble.

CHAPTER THIRTEEN

Illustrative Material

No program is like any other. You must always try to adapt your introductions to the needs of the occasion, but the following may prove useful in devising announcements of your own.

An Annual Banquet

The first example is typical but mythical — the annual convention banquet of the state association of hardware dealers. You will readily see that, with slight adaptation, the material can be used to fit almost any situation of a similar sort.

The Opening: Good evening, ladies and gentlemen. I am your master of ceremonies. I am very ill equipped for the job I have in hand because I know absolutely nothing about the hardware business. However, since I'm also your toastmaster, it seems appropriate that I should pop-up anyway.

I realize that's sort of a gun, but I understand that puns are better that way—when they're toasted.

But enough of this prittle-prattle! You have the right to know who I am. I am _____. Ordinarily, I make my living by _____. Tonight, as your toastmaster, I hope to keep everything crisp and done to a turn.

There's one thing about an occasion like this — that's the passage of time. It's been one year since the previous meeting of this august body. All of us are a little older and presumably a little wiser. That's one thing we can't hurry — the passage of time. Especially between paydays.

Nevertheless, on behalf of your association, I am happy to welcome you to this, your annual convention banquet, and express the sincere hope that you enjoy yourselves. At the price of the tickets, you had better! Actually, I think the committee has done a pretty fair job. There have been banquets where I not only rose to speak after I had been served, but I went away muttering for days afterward.

I would like at this time to introduce the distinguished chairman of the committee on banquet arrangements and invite you to applaud him heartily for his efforts on your behalf. He is _____ of _____.

Introduction of Guests: In addition to the chairman of the committee on arrangements, we have a number of other very distinguished guests. We have them all up here at the head table where we can keep an eye on them.

An expert has been defined as any reasonably intelligent person who is away from home. Since all of these people up here at the head table are experts, it is presumed that they are also away from home — which is another reason we want to keep an eye on them.

The first person we want to introduce is the expiring president of your organization. I say "expiring" advisedly, because I understand he just barely made it.

Usually, after a man has spent a year as the president of an association like yours, he ends up bent and broken. Or he just ends up. If he's bent and broken, he's done a good job. If not, . . . Well, your ex-president is a very modest man and says he's had a lot of good help and, besides, he says that after having spent twenty-five years in the hardware business, he can stand anything. Your ex-president, _____.

When introducing the ladies at an affair of this kind, it is customary to dig up a quantity of adjectives like "charming," "winsome" and the like. However, in this case, it is not necessary to dig very far. They spring naturally to the lips. The wife of your ex-president, _____.

We turn now from the past to the future. Since we have done honor to your immediate past president, there is no reason at all why we shouldn't do the same thing for the one who is to serve in the year ahead.

Before we introduce him, though, there is one thing that ought to be remembered. Regardless of what has happened to him, regardless of the honors that have already been bestowed, he is not responsible. His wife is. He told me that himself — and she told him.

The wife of your new president, _____.

It is customary these days to look into the future with fear and trembling. With the new president of your association, it is not necessary to fear — just tremble. As a matter of fact, we think he got everything he deserves. When he stood up before this organization and it was announced that he was to be your new president for the next twelve months, he said, "Thank you, judge! That's the shortest sentence I ever got!"

Your new president, _____.

Music: Assembling suitable music for a group of hardware merchants presents something of a problem. We did not know how many music lovers there were among you. By the way, you know what a music lover is, don't you? A music lover is one who when a beautiful girl is singing in the bathtub places his ear against the keyhole. Tonight, I am happy to say that our music is as easy on the eyes as it is on the ears. We have Miss _____, of _____, who will sing _____.

Presentation of Gifts: This annual banquet, like Christmas, comes but once a year, but it has other features which are also similar. One of these is the appearance of Santa Claus. Minus beard, he now comes down the chimney in the person of

_____.

(As suggested in the text, the person thus introduced goes on to make the actual presentation. In a case of this kind, the master of ceremonies must be careful not to steal any thunder from the person making the presentation.)

The Main Speech: Through this entire evening, I've been trying to think of a joke about the hardware business but haven't come up with one yet. After all, I guess the hardware business is no joke — especially around inventory time. Which does remind me of a little story of the hardware merchant who did lose his mind during inventory time one year and was sent off to the state insane asylum. His recovery was slow because, when he got there, they set him to counting the nuts in his new abode. They figured he had experience.

However, he doesn't mind. He feels he'll be crazy enough to make a success of the hardware business when he gets out again.

I don't think anyone can fail to be impressed by the tremendous strides made by the hardware business in the past few years. Methods of merchandising and the merchandise itself have all changed to make the merchant of greater service to the customer.

One of the men who has been instrumental in making many of these changes is our speaker tonight. As chairman in charge of the Program and Promotions Committee of the national association, he has seen to it that the latest and best in new store ideas have been available to the entire country. I am sure that we are grateful for the opportunity to hear of his experiences at first-hand and to learn what he thinks of the year ahead.

"Looking Forward" is the name of his talk, and I think that title keys his whole approach to the hardware business. Mr. _____.

* * * * *

Closing Announcement: Our thanks to you, Mr. _____ _____, for a lively and interesting subject well presented. We shall look forward to your appearance at possible future conventions of this association.

Good-nights should be brief unless, of course, you are under twenty-five and alone on the front porch with a beautiful girl. Since I am neither young nor beautiful nor a girl, I shall be as brief as possible.

The committee wishes me to thank you, one and all, for your attendance here tonight. The members hope you have had a good time and that the program has been worth your while.

Before closing, I have been also asked to announce that the convention dance, to the music of Elmer Johnson and His Jitterbugs, will begin immediately after the tables are cleared.

Thank you and good-night!

A Useful Theme

Using a theme to tie together the diverse elements of the banquet program was discussed in the text. The following are useful examples that with minor variations can be used in many different circumstances.

The Opening: Good evening, ladies and gentlemen. I am your announcer. Normally, I would be your toastmaster or your master of ceremonies but, tonight, we are doing things a bit differently. We are carrying out a theme in the presentation of our banquet program. That theme is radio.

We chose radio because we have a number of loudspeakers here. We may not be good, but we will be loud.

Of course, after we had chosen radio as our theme, we did have some difficulty in deciding on the particular kind of program. It couldn't be a quiz — that would be too questionable. We thought once of having a soap opera; it would make a good clean show, but we thought someone might be drowned in the tears. So, we decided to keep it a mystery. That way, we can get away with murder.

Before you decide to switch over to another station, I'd like to say that we're very happy to see such a large crowd here tonight. It proves that radio is here to stay and why aren't you home listening to it?

I did have a few electrical stories with which to open this program, but most of them are too shocking. We'll get right on with the first number.

The Music: We did want to get a few radio stars here tonight, but we had difficulty finding some that would suit our purposes. We thought of Big Crosby; his voice is too low. We thought of the Andrews Sisters, but there are too many of them. Every leading radio star we considered — there was something wrong. Mostly the fact that they all wanted too much money. We finally compromised by finding someone who would appear for two cereal box-tops and an old worn-out phonograph record. For our first musical tonight, we are going to hear _____.

* * * * *

Earlier in our program, I made some crack about our inability to get some leading radio stars because we couldn't pay enough money. That really isn't so. We were willing a pay almost any amount of money to get good entertainment here tonight, but we did have difficulty getting someone from the field of radio. Most of them said they never heard of us before. Also some of them said they were afraid to appear before a live audience. A live audience! This audience is alive? They should stand where I am. Nevertheless, as the second musical number on our program tonight, we are to hear _____.

Presentation of Guests: A moment ago I said something about not having a quiz on our program tonight. I was wrong. Perhaps, we should have one. I say that because we do have some very questionable characters here tonight. We have even had trouble deciding in what categories they belong. Rather than explore this matter any further, however, I do think it advisable to proceed with the introduction of a number of distinguished guests we have with us this evening.

(Proceeds by giving the name and title or any other useful information about those who are to be introduced)

*　　*　　*　　*　　*

Announcements: No radio program is complete without a commercial. You know, rip off the head of your mother-in-law and send it in just to get rid of it. We wanted you to feel at home while listening to this program tonight, so we have decided to throw in a few commercials.

(Goes ahead with making such necessary announcements as he has been asked to include on the program, such as where the payment of dues can be made.)

*　　*　　*　　*　　*

Community Singing: You know, on the radio, they have what is known as an audience participation show. That is a show where the audience provides the entertainment but somebody else gets paid for it.

Right now, we're going to have a little audience participation. We're going to ask you to engage in some community singing.

Personally, I think the human race is divided into two kinds of people — those who like community singing and those who don't. Or let's put it another way, those who can sing and those who can't.

I like to sing; it sounds so good when I stop. It sounds better yet if I never even start.

That being true, I'm going to introduce you again to a friend of yours, a solid citizen with leather lungs and a golden voice. Here he is now, _____.

* * * * *

The Main Speech: As the climax to most radio programs, they usually present a sketch. So I guess this is where our resemblance to radio ends. Our speaker tonight is scarcely a sketch; he is a full length portrait.

Actually, we went to considerable trouble to provide a main event on our program tonight. Since this is sort of a radio program, we thought of a give-away — a chance to win a refrigerator or twenty-eight thousand dollars and forty-two cents simply for guessing the mystery melody. In the end, however, we decided to be different merely by providing an effective speech.

They tell me that on the radio when the average speaker is presented, most of his listeners tune him out. You are not so lucky. Whatever happens from this point on, you have got to sit there and take it.

Fortunately, there are exceptions. Our speaker tonight is one of them. No one would think of tuning him out, whatever the occasion.

* * * * *

(Goes on to introduce the speaker in greater personal detail as suggested in the text.)

Closing: We have reached the end. In a radio station, this is called the sign-off. You will, doubtless, recall the story of the mattress company that sponsored the silence between a station's sign-off at night and its sign-on the following morning. I will gladly sell the time between now and next year's convention to anyone interested for a dollar-and-a-half.

Regardless of monetary consideration, we trust that you have found this year's stay at your annual convention both pleasurable and profitable. On behalf of the committee in charge, I have been asked to express their thanks for your support of the various programs offered and to express the hope that you have found it sufficiently worthwhile to already plan on attending next year.

Thanks and good-night!

*   *   *   *   *

A Vaudeville Show

These short squibs may help you if you are called upon to introduce different kinds of variety acts. They show you the terseness and comic content of this type of introduction.

Dog Act: They say a dog is man's best friend. No one has ever consulted the dog about it. Who knows? He may prefer another dog. I know what I would do if I were a dog. I'd take another dog in preference to some of the people I know. All of which goes to show that not only is a dog man's best friend, but he is also smarter. To prove it, here is _____ _____.

Acrobats: They tell me that acrobats are the only people who can turn a flop into a success. Of course, to be a good acrobat, one has to make a successful flop. On the other hand, why bother? Personally, I have never cared for exercise. I took some once and look at me now. Right now, we're going to present some hand-to-hand balancing. They also tell me that the boys got their heads together and came up with a pretty good act. The _____.

*   *   *   *   *

Male Quartette: Now, I'm going to introduce four boys. They call themselves a quartette, but that's only because one of them can count. None of them claim to be singers but, by doing it together, they also say they have a tendency to drown each other out. That's what makes a good quartette. Now, if they'd only drown together. No, they're still a good quartette. The _____.

*   *   *   *   *

Magician: When I came into this place tonight, I was comparatively wealthy. I had a dollar-and-a-half. I loaned it to a fellow backstage. He says he's a magician. He must be. He told me he was going to show me how to take what I earn and make it cover my expenses. I know this much, though: I haven't seen that dollar-and-a-half since I talked to him. If that's what it takes to be a magician, I think I'll apply for the job. Here he is _____.

* * * * *

A Student Recital

Customarily, a printed program is provided at recital programs, but not always. Sometimes, such programs are too expensive or prove impractical for other reasons. When that happens, announcements similar to the one below can be used in introducing the various students who appear on the program.

The second young lady who appears on the program this evening is Miss Doris Cook, who is twelve years old. She has been studying the piano for twelve years and, in that time, has made considerable progress. She is the daughter of Mr. and Mrs. Fred Cook, of Grover City. Miss Cook will play a group of three numbers—Mignonette, Dancing Clown, and Morning.

* * * * *

An Amateur Show

As indicated in the text, amateurs, when introduced on the radio or in person, can be interviewed to bring out their capabilities. A perusal of the following, for form and content, might prove helpful:

Emcee: And now, our next contestant—Ferdinand Black of Hill City. Good evening. Is that what they call you?

Contestant: Most of the time they call me Freddie.

Emcee: O.K., Freddie. How long have you been playing that squeeze-box of yours?

Contestant: About three years.

Emcee: What made you decide to take up the accordion?

Contestant: I started out playing the piano, but it was too hard to carry around. So I decided to take up the accordion.

Emcee: You're something of a comedian, too, I see. Have you ever taken lessons on your instrument?

Contestant: Oh, yes. I've been studying about two years— with Vincent Alessandro. I've just won a scholarship and that entitles me to lessons for the next year.

Emcee: That's wonderful! Congratulations, Freddie, and let's see how you do when you play — Twelfth Street Rag! Freddie Black!

*   *   *   *   *

Extensible Stories

In addition to the example contained in the text, here are a number of extensible stories. They are not particularly original; they have been around for years but, if you use them judiciously, you will find that audiences enjoy them immensely.

*   *   *   *   *

Once upon a time, there was a little fly. He kept buzzing and buzzing around until, one bright and sunny day, he came to the door of a butcher shop. He kept buzzing around but, try as he might, he couldn't get into the shop. Inside, he could smell some fine bologna, and he wanted some the worst way, for the little fly was very, very hungry. So, he kept buzzing around and around and around. At last, a little old lady came tottering down the street and went into the shop and he was able to sneak his way in. Happily the little fly went buzzing around and around until he found the bologna, and he ate his fill. My goodness, he felt good! Never in his life could he remember feeling better. Taking wing, he went buzzing and buzzing around the shop, flying hither and yon. One day to hither, the next to yon. Finally, the butcher could stand it no longer. He picked up a swatter and killed the little fly dead as dead can be, which only goes to prove the moral of our story: When you're full of bologna, don't go buzzing around!

*   *   *   *   *

Once upon a time, there was a magician who had a parrot as his best friend and severest critic. The parrot was a nice bird in every way, but he had one bad habit. Every time the magician performed a trick, he — the parrot, that is — would yell, "Fake! Fake! Fake!" This habit, as you can imagine, tended to irritate the magician, and so he decided to perfect a new disappearing act that would completely flabbergast the parrot. The magician started out with rabbits, making them disappear, but when the parrot saw the trick, all he would yell was, "Fake! Fake! Fake!" The magician improved the trick.

He got dogs to disappear. Again the parrot yelled, "Fake! Fake! Fake" He worked up to a donkey, but still the parrot kept on yelling. Finally, the magician could stand it no longer. He got so he could make an elephant disappear, but the parrot kept right on yelling, "Fake! Fake! Fake!" The magician was beginning to get very angry, indeed, but he decided to continue with the trick regradless of the opinion of the parrot and, because he was so sensationally successful with everyone except his feathery friend. Eventually the magician got invited overseas where he was to perform before the crowned heads of Europe. On the way, his ship struck a floating mine and was sunk. The parrot managed to land on a floating life raft, but it was some time before the magician succeeded in swimming from the depths of the sea to join him. As the magician surfaced, he discovered that the parrot was standing on the raft scanning the horizon in every direction but nowhere could he find the boat. Finally, he turned to the magician and said, "All right, I give up! Where is it?"

* * * * *

A friend of mine was in show business. He had been remarkably prosperous. So it surprised me one day when I met him coming down the street looking like a veritable bum. "What's the matter?" I asked. "It's a sad story," he said. "Come into this bar and I'll tell you all about it." Over his drink, my friend told me one of the saddest tales of woe I have ever heard. It seems that my friend at one time had one of the most sensationally successful animal acts that had ever been presented before the American public. He had a dog who could sing and a monkey who could play the piano. He went everywhere, appearing in theatres from coast to coast, on the radio and in television and, finally, in the movies. The dog would sing and the monkey would accompany him on the piano. The act, as I say, was a tremendous success but, at last, my friend said, "They caught up with me. You know," he said, "That dog was a fake. He couldn't sing at all. The monkey was a ventriloquist!"

* * * * *

Once there were two gnus. (Pronounced for the purposes

of this joke as "guh-new.") One was named Emily and the other Archibald. Since one was obviously a boy gnu and the other a girl gnu, they decided to get married, and so they did. They lived very happily on the African plains until, one day, as such things will, they happened to get a little gnu. His name was Elmer. He grew and grew. Eventually, Emily and Archibald awoke to the discovery that their little Elmer was no longer a little gnu but was getting bigger and bigger and was beginning to go out with other gnus. They also discovered that when he was out on Saturday night he was doing a lot of things that he shouldn't have. This perturbed Emily and Archibald. Said Emily to Archibald, "You're going to have to do something about this." "Oh, no," said Archibald to Emily, "Elmer is your problem. You're going to have to chastise him and see to it that he keeps from running around at night." "Oh, no," said Emily to Archibald, "That's your job. You paddle your own gnu!"

*   *   *   *   *

The Forum

The term "forum" sounds somewhat forbidding. Yet, you will be called upon to introduce a forum more often than you might think. Any meeting where a series of speakers discourse on different phases of a single subject can properly be called a forum.

Roughly, you must introduce the subject, then introduce the various speakers who are going to handle it. You must try to relate the subject to the needs of the listeners and then show how the different speakers are qualified to discuss the separate parts.

Here is how it might be done at a Parents-Teachers' Association meeting designed to consider the construction of a new schoolhouse:

The Opening: Good evening. We are happy to see such a large crowd here tonight.

This meeting has been called for the purpose of considering the construction of a new school building in School District One. It has been called under the auspices of the Parent-Teacher's Association in order that the parents and friends of the district might have an opportunity to learn what has been and what is being planned in the way of a new schoolhouse.

As you know, this subject has been under consideration for some time. Discussion started about six months ago when the latest school census disclosed the fact that the recent growth of population in this district is going to make the present structure entirely inadequate.

Steps have been taken to place this question on the ballot in the next school election, but this meeting has been called to allow you to learn the reasons for this move and to ask any questions that you may have.

We have three speakers here tonight, each of them equipped to handle separate phases of the subject under consideration. The first of these is Mr. _____, our local superintendent of schools. He is the one who instigated the school survey last summer and who has the facts at his finger-tips. Mr. _____.

(The first speaker outlines the basic need for the new structure. He gives what is in essence an historical survey of the need. After he finishes, the moderator goes on to introduce the second speaker.)

Thank you, Mr. _____. After listening to your resumé of the facts brought out in the school survey, I think you can understand the reasons for the next step which has been taken. In order to place this question on the ballot, certain legal requirements must be met. To explain what they are, we have been fortunate tonight in securing the services of our city attorney, Mr. _____, who will explain this part of the procedure. Mr. _____.

(He carries on the subject to the final phase which is action by the audience. The third speaker can be introduced by the moderator in a manner something like the following.)

We have heard two phases of the work necessary to get a new school building in this district. There is still a third — what we as citizens can do to make this plan a reality. To discuss this third and final phase, we have Mrs. _____, president of the Parent-Teachers' Association. Mrs. _____ has been associated with this

plan from the beginning and is prepared now to tell us what can be expected from all of us in the future. Mrs. _____
_____.

(After the third and final talk, the last stage of the meeting might go on as follows.)

You have heard the proposal for a new schoolhouse discussed from every possible angle. Yet, you still may have questions about the project. We are prepared to answer them now. To begin, I am going to ask that questions be restricted one to a person. Then, after all having had an opportunity to be heard, we can go back to some of those remaining unanswered.

(Carries the question period through to its end.)

* * * * *

Jokes

It's always a problem to know what to do at a time like this. One never knows whether to let your audience enjoy themselves or to start with the speeches.

* * * * *

I remember one time when I told a story like that they threw me out the back door. I protested. After all, I told them, I'm rather an important fellow, and that's no way to be treated. So, they invited me back in again and threw me out the front door.

* * * * *

It's always well, on occasions of this kind, to be brief as possible. I remember one time when I had rambled on a bit longer than usual, a man—a friend of mine—reminded me of it after the meeting was over. I told him I was very sorry but that I had forgotten my watch and had left it home. He told me that I shouldn't have worried; there was a calendar on the wall behind me.

Working at banquets, as I frequently do, reminds me of the story about Egbert, the Egg King. Egbert, the Egg King, applied for a job with one of our better traveling carnivals. "What do you do?" the owner asked him. "Well," said Egbert, "To start out, I eat a dozen hen's eggs. After that, I eat a few goose eggs and, after that, I finish off with a great big ostrich egg." "That's fine," the owner told him, "When can you start?" "Now," said Egbert. "Remember," the owner reminded him, "in this show, we do between eight and ten performances a day." "I'm sorry," said Egbert, "I can't work for you. I've got to have time for my regular meals."

* * * * *

The committee in charge of this banquet has been very efficient. They remind me of the doctor who struggled out into the country to see a patient whose wife had called him. When he got there, the wife was very profuse in her thanks. "Oh, that's all right," said the doctor. "I had another patient in this neighborhood anyway. I thought I'd kill two birds with one stone."

* * * * *

It is part of the job of a master of ceremonies to know some hair-raising stories. Which reminds me of the one about the man who went out to get a haircut on company time. The boss told him he wasn't supposed to do that. "Why not?" the man asked. "It grew on company time." And speaking of hair, a friend of mine went to a doctor. He asked him how to avoid falling hair. The doctor told him to get out from under it. Of course, women have trouble with hair, too. A friend's wife asked him if he would still love her when her hair had turned to gray. He said, "Why not?" He had loved her when it had been every other color.

* * * * *

Glossary of Terms

Act—Dramatically, a division of a play. In vaudeville terms, a separate part of the program. A single dance may be an act. So is a group of three which appears as a unit. In this sense, used as a noun.

Afterpiece—An entertainment presented after a main part. Specifically, the second half of a minstrel show, when it is sometimes called an olio.

Ad lib—In plays, to speak extemporaneously lines which are not in the script. By extension, in radio or television, to speak extemporaneously without a script at all.

Amplifier—That part of the public address system which multiplies or enlarges the electronic impulses sent into it. For all practical purposes, it enlarges the volume of sound spoken into a microphone. The quantity of that sound is controlled by a "volume control," usually so marked on the panel of the amplifier.

Audience Participation—A program where the audience acts as a part of the entertainment without previous rehearsal.

Cabaret—A style of entertainment where the program is presented with the audience on all four sides or on three. Usually a vaudeville or variety show as opposed to a dramatic program.

Cold—In radio parlance, appearing without benefit of a previous introduction by music, either fanfare or theme. The voice introduced without music.

Continuity—The order of the program. The typed script which contains the order of the program and the announcements used to introduce the various parts.

Debate—A formal argument in which two opposing speakers are allowed an equal amount of time in which to present their arguments and in which time is allowed for rebuttal. Usually, only two sides of any question are debated.

Emcee—From the initial letters M. C., designating a master of ceremonies. Refers to the person and to the act of being an emcee.

Extemporaneous—Without benefit of prepared text. Most good so-called extemporaneous speeches are very carefully thought out in advance. No good speaker rises to his feet without some idea of what he expects to say.

First Part—The first act of a minstrel, characterized by repartee between the two end men and the Interlocutor. The performers sit in a semi-circle with the end men closest to the audience at each end of the arc and with the Interlocutor seated farthest away at the apex of the arc.

Forum—A speaking program on which a series of speakers talk about the same general subject or different phases of the same general subject.

Free Act—A circus or vaudeville act which appears in front of the grandstand at an afternoon performance of a fair, celebration or rodeo. At a street fair or carnival, any outside act presented without admission may be called a free act.

Gag—A short joke complete in itself as opposed to situation comedy which is built around a comic set of circumstances.

Gimmick—Originally, a method of controlling the action of wheels at a carnival. Now, in radio or television, any method of adding to the complications in a quiz or audience participation show. A trick method.

Horn—Name for the speaker on a public address system.

Interlocutor—The master of ceremonies of a minstrel show.

Live Audience—In radio or television, the audience which is actually present in the studio at the time of the broadcast or telecast as opposed to the audience listening or viewing in the home.

M. C.—Contraction for master of ceremonies.

Master of Ceremonies—A person who introduces or conducts any program and who provides the continuity between the members of that program.

Microphone—An instrument for converting sound waves into electrical impulses so that they can be amplified.

Moderator—The master of ceremonies of a panel or round-table discussion.

Number—An individual part or section of a vaudeville or variety show.

Olio—The afterpiece of a minstrel show. Also any entertainment presented as an afterpiece, as a vaudeville show presented after an old-time melodrama. Sometimes, any act presented before an olio or drop at the forepart of the stage.

"P. A." System—Contraction for public address system. A system for taking sound waves, converting them into electric impulses, amplifying them, and then, re-converting them into sound waves of a greater volume.

Panel Discussion—A discussion on which the members of the panel are presumed to be experts in their own particular fields.

Quiz-Master—The master of ceremonies of a quiz show.

Quiz Show—An audience participation show of which the principal ingredient is the asking of questions by the master of ceremonies or quiz-master.

Reaction—Return action or response. Dramatically, the facial reaction or expression or gesture that one gives in reply to a previous speech or situation.

Roundtable Discussion—A discussion in which the participants need not be experts representing a particular viewpoint.

Routine—As a noun, the order of a program or the order of the parts in a single act of a program. As a verb, the act of devising such an order.

Segue—A musical term. Going from one musical number to another without a break.

Semi-Finish—A climax of an act, usually acrobatic, which is not the conclusion. After a semi-finish, the performers come out again, increase the applause getting potentialities of their tricks and then conclude.

Showmanship—The art of making any program or entertainment more acceptable to an audience.

Slow Take—A reaction which is slow in coming.

Sound System—Another name for a public address system.

Speaker—Another name for the horns of a sound system.

Specialty—When referring to a master of ceremonies, an act performed in addition to his regular duties, as singing, dancing, or magic.

Stage Left—That part of the stage which lies to the left of the performer as opposed to the audience. Stage Left is on the audience's right.

Stage Right—Opposite of the above.

Straight Man—A person who asks questions of a comedian so that the latter can give funny answers and who then reacts in such a way as to increase the quantity of an audience's laughter.

Timing—The art of telling stories, saying lines or performing actions in such a way that the maximum in entertainment value is achieved. Based upon an understanding of audiences and their ability to comprehend what is performed before them.

Toastmaster—A master of ceremonies who appears at a banquet or luncheon.

Vaudeville—Entertainment made up of a variety of different types of acts as singing, dancing, juggling or acrobatics.